Capitol Cuisine

Capitol Cuisine

Recipes from the Hill

A Bipartisan Cookbook

DIANE MILLIKEN

W. W. NORTON & COMPANY
NEW YORK   LONDON

The Banana Bread recipe submitted by Senator John Chafee is from *The Blender Cookbook* by Anne Seranne and Eileen Gadon (New York: Doubleday, 1961). Reprinted with the permission of Eileen Gadon.

The Chicken Velvet Soup and Wild Rice and Mushrooms recipe submitted by Representative George R. Nethercutt, Jr., is from *Gallery Buffett Soup Cookbook, Revised Fourth Edition* (Dallas: Dallas Museum of Art League, 1983). Reprinted with the permission of the Dallas Museum of Art League.

The Pasta Frittata recipe submitted by Congresswoman Patricia Schroeder is from *Southern Living Cookbook: From the Foods Staff of Southern Living Magazine*, edited by Susan Carlisle Payne. Copyright © 1995 by Oxmoor House. Reprinted by permission.

The text of this book is composed in Fournier
with the display set in Futura and Party
Composition and manufacturing by The Maple-Vail Book Manufacturing Group
Book design by Chris Welch

Library of Congress Cataloging-in-Publication Data
Milliken, Diane.
Capitol cuisine : recipes from the Hill : a bipartisan cookbook /
by Diane Milliken.
p.   cm.
Includes index.
ISBN 0-393-31579-7 (pbk.)
1. Cookery, American.   2. Politicians—United States.   I. Title.
TX715.M649   1996
641.5973—dc20   96-13300
CIP

W. W. Norton & Company, Inc., 500 Fifth Avenue, New York, N.Y. 10110
http://web.wwnorton.com

W. W. Norton & Company Ltd., 10 Coptic Street, London WC1A 1PU

1 2 3 4 5 6 7 8 9 0

To Rich and Jesse, I love you both!

Contents

Preface   x v i i
Acknowledgments   x i x

residential and Vice-Presidential Dishes

Hillary Clinton's Chocolate Chips ★ *Hillary Clinton*   3

Tennessee Treats ★ *Tipper Gore*   4

Barbecued Chicken ★ *Barbara Bush*   5

Red, White, and Blue Cobbler ★ *Barbara Bush*   7

Cole Slaw ★ *Barbara Bush*   9

Monkey Bread ★ *Nancy Reagan*   1 0

Cream of Broccoli Soup, with No Cream ★ *Rosalynn Carter*   1 1

Blu'Bana Bread ★ *Betty Ford*   1 2

Shrimp-Squash Casserole ★ *Lady Bird Johnson*   1 3

Peach Cobbler ★ *Marilyn Quayle*   1 4

Salted Nut Bars ★ *Joan Mondale*   1 5

Spaghetti Sauce ★ *Judy Agnew*   1 6

Grape Juice Fruit Ice ★ *Judy Agnew*   1 7

𝓑eef 𝓓ishes

Lite and Lean Beef Broil ★ *Senator Larry E. Craig*   2 1

Wild Rice Stew ★ *Senator Bob Packwood*   2 2

Dakota Bean Salad ★ *Senator Larry Pressler*   2 3

Dakota Bean Stew ★ *Senator Larry Pressler*   2 4

Keftedes (Greek Meatballs) ★ *Representative Michael Bilirakis*   2 5

Marinated Eye of the Round ★ *Representative Charlie Rose*   2 6

South Dakota Taco Salad ★ *Senator Tom Daschle*   2 7

Swedish Meatballs ★ *Representative Charles Stenholm*   2 8

"Bohemian" Teriyaki Beef ★ *Senator J. James Exon*   2 9

Exon Family Favorite Casserole ★ *Senator J. James Exon*   3 0

𝓟oultry 𝓓ishes

Oriental Chicken Salad ★ *Senator David Pryor*   3 3

Peachy Chicken ★ *Senator Connie Mack*   3 4

J. Bennett Johnston's Favorite Chicken Salad ★

Senator J. Bennett Johnston   3 5

Chicken Caruso and Rice ★ *Senator John Kerry*   3 6

Garlic-Chicken Phyllo Rolls ★ *Representative Calvin Dooley*   3 7

Chicken Tetrazzini ★ *Senator Howell Heflin*   3 9

Mrs. Sheila Wellstone's Curried Chicken ★ *Senator Paul David Wellstone*   4 0

Grilled Pesto-Stuffed Chicken with Lemon Butter ★

Representative Bill Archer   4 1

Chicken Breast Dinner ★ *Senator Paul D. Coverdell*   4 2

Sweet and Sour Chicken (Low-Fat) ★ *Senator Robert F. Bennett*   4 3

Chicken Scallopini ★ *Senator Alfonse D'Amato*   4 4

Fruited Chicken Salad ★ *Representative Steve Largent*   4 5

Marty Meehan's Chicken Picatta ★ *Representative Marty Meehan*   4 6

Honey-Mustard Chicken ★ *Senator Frank Lautenberg*   4 7

Dottie Miller's Oriental Chicken ★ *Representative Dave Weldon*   4 8

Amy Adam's Lemon Chicken ★ *Representative Dave Weldon*   4 9

Korean Chicken ★ *Senator Daniel K. Akaka*   5 0

Lime and Cilantro Grilled Turkey Breast in Pita Pockets ★

Senator Richard Lugar   5 1

Dove on the Grill ★ *Senator Richard Shelby*   5 3

Pork and Lamb Dishes

Christmas Tortière (Pork Pie) ★ *Diane Milliken (author)*   5 7

Sweet-Sour Spareribs ★ *Senator Daniel K. Akaka*   5 8

Pork Chops and Spanish Rice ★ *Representative Henry B. Gonzalez*   5 9

Pepper Pork Chops ★ *Senator Alfonse D'Amato*   6 1

Pork Roast ★ *Representative Doug Bereuter*   6 2

Stuffed Iowa Pork Chops ★ *Senator Tom Harkin*   6 3

Braised or Broiled Pork Chops ★ *Senator Lauch Faircloth*   6 4

Roast Leg of Spring Lamb ★ *Senator Rick Santorum*   6 5

Fish and Seafood Dishes

Fish Dijon ★ *Senator Connie Mack*   6 9

Sautéed Trout with Fresh Tarragon ★ *Senator Daniel Patrick Moynihan*   7 0

Catfish Casserole ★ *Senator Trent Lott*   7 1

Red Snapper ★ *Senator Sam Nunn*   7 2

San Francisco Seasoned Shrimp ★ *Senator Dianne Feinstein*   7 3

Seville Shrimp ★ *Senator Bob Dole*   7 4

Garithes Me Lemoni Ke Lathee (Shrimp with Lemon and Olive Oil) ★
Representative Michael Bilirakis   7 5

Frank's Favorite Scallops ★ *Senator Frank H. Murkowski*   7 6

John Warner's Norfolk Crab Cakes ★ *Senator John Warner*   7 7

Baked Shad and Roe ★ *Senator William V. Roth, Jr.*   7 8

Sautéed Shrimp and Scallops ★ *Senator Rick Santorum*   7 9

Vegetable Dishes

Texas Potatoes ★ *Representative Barbara Cubin*   8 3

Hash Brown Casserole ★ *Representative Tom Latham*   8 4

Potatoes à la Bernice ★ *Senator Dirk Kempthorne*   8 5

Tamale Corn ★ *Representative Barbara Cubin*   8 6

Spanakopita (Spinach Pie) ★ *Representative Michael Bilirakis*   8 7

Stuffed Cabbage ★ *Senator Carl Levin*   8 8

French-Cut String Beans ★ *Senator Alfonse D'Amato*   8 9

Beets in Sour Cream Sauce ★ *Representative Philip M. Crane*   9 0

Beans and Rice

Hoppin' John ★ *Senator Mitch McConnell*   9 3

Arizona Baked Beans ★ *Senator John McCain*   9 4

Phil Gramm's Award-Winning Chili ★ *Senator Phil Gramm*   9 5

Cincinnati Chili ★ *Representative Michael G. Oxley*   9 6

Baked Lima Beans ★ *Senator Jesse Helms*   9 7

Searchlight Beans and Rice ★ *Senator Harry Reid*   9 8

Wild Rice and Mushrooms ★ *Representative George R. Nethercutt, Jr.*   9 9

Grandma Daigle's Rice Dressing ★ *Senator John Breaux*   1 0 0

Pistachio Rice Pilaf ★ *Senator Joseph Lieberman*   1 0 1

Baked Rice ★ *Senator Alfonse D'Amato*   1 0 2

Salads

Strawberry-Spinach Salad ★ *Representative John A. Boehner*   1 0 5

Vegetable Salad ★ *Senator Sam Nunn*   1 0 6

Broccoli Salad ★ *Senator Bob Smith*   1 0 7

Breads

The Grassley Family's Favorite Corn Bread ★ *Senator Charles E. Grassley*   1 1 1

Easy Corn Bread ★ *Representative Michael G. Oxley*   1 1 2

Georgia Peach Bread Recipe ★ *Senator Sam Nunn*   1 1 3

Quick and Easy Banana Bread ★ *Senator John H. Chafee*   1 1 4

Swedish Rye Bread ★ *Representative Charles W. Stenholm*   1 1 5

Zucchini Nut Bread ★ *Representative Sam Brownback*   1 1 6

Pasta Dishes

Pizza Casserole ★ *Representative James B. Longley, Jr.*   1 1 9

Pasta Frittata ★ *Representative Pat Schroeder*   1 2 0

Lasagna ★ *Senator Alfonse D'Amato*   1 2 1

Sherry's Spaghetti Sauce and Meatballs ★ *Representative Sherwood Boehlert*   1 2 2

Extra-Meaty Lasagna ★ *Senator Kent Conrad*   1 2 3

xii

★

Contents

Soups and Chowders

Instant Meatball Soup ★ *Senator Alfonse D'Amato*   1 2 7

Lentil Soup ★ *Senator Alfonse D'Amato*   1 2 8

Charleston She-Crab Soup ★ *Senator Ernest F. Hollings*   1 2 9

The Famous Senate Restaurant Bean Soup ★ *Senator Carl Levin*   1 3 0

Squash Soup ★ *Representative Steve Stockman*   1 3 1

Missouri Apple Soup ★ *Senator Christopher Bond*   1 3 2

Potato-Dill Soup ★ *Senator Daniel Patrick Moynihan*   1 3 3

Chicken Velvet Soup ★ *Representative George R. Nethercutt, Jr.*   1 3 4

Dale's Crab Soup ★ *Senator Dale Bumpers*   1 3 5

Grape Soup ★ *Representative John W. Olver*   1 3 6

Clam Chowder ★ *Senator John H. Chafee*   1 3 8

Rhode Island Clam Chowder ★ *Senator Claiborne Pell*   1 3 9

Easy Hearty Corn Chowder ★ *Senator Kay Bailey Hutchison*   1 4 0

Ted Kennedy's Cape Cod Fish Chowder ★ *Senator Ted Kennedy*   1 4 1

Brunch Dishes

Aunt Evelyn's Johnnycake or Muffins ★ *Senator John H. Chafee*   1 4 5

Swedish Pancakes ★ *Senator Patty Murray*   1 4 6

Dentist's Dream French Toast ★ *Representative Joseph P. Kennedy II*   1 4 7

Mom's English Scones ★ *Senator James Inhofe*   1 4 8

Giant Apple Popovers ★ *Senator Arlen Specter*   1 4 9

Appetizers and Dips

Miniature Ham Rolls ★ *Senator Strom Thurmond*   1 5 3

Josefinas ★ *Representative John T. Myers*   1 5 4

Cheese Straws ★ *Senator Howell Heflin*   1 5 5

Hot Chicken Wings à la Thomas ★ *Senator Craig Thomas*   1 5 6

Tostada Grande ★ *Representative John T. Myers*   1 5 7

Hot Crab-Artichoke Dip ★ *Representative John T. Myers*   1 5 8

Garbanzo Dip ★ *Senator Sam Nunn*   1 5 9

Hot Crab Dip ★ *Representative John T. Myers*   1 6 0

Miscellaneous

Liz Bryant's Coffee Punch ★ *Representative Dave Weldon*   1 6 3

Indian Green Chutney ★ *Senator Arlen Specter*   1 6 4

Sesame Dressing ★ *Representative John T. Myers*   1 6 5

Crème Fraîche ★ *Senator James Inhofe*   1 6 6

Desserts

Fruit Desserts

Fruit Crunch ★ *Senator Ernest F. Hollings*   1 6 9

Curried Fruit ★ *Representative Ralph M. Hall*   1 7 0

Apple Crumble ★ *Senator Paul Sarbanes*   1 7 1

Baked Apples ★ *Senator John D. Rockefeller IV*   1 7 2

Cakes

Banana-Pineapple Cake ★ *Representative Steven Schiff*   1 7 3

Cherry Nut Bread ★ *Representative Tim Johnson*   1 7 4

Our Family Gingerbread ★ *Senator Bob Smith*   1 7 5

Ruth Thompson's Fresh Coconut Cake, with Fluffy White Frosting ★
Senator Fred Thompson   1 7 6

Maple Syrup Cake ★ *Senator Jim Jeffords*   1 7 8

Deep Dark Chocolate Cake ★ *Representative Sam Brownback*   1 7 9

Chocolate Huckleberry Layer Cake ★ *Senator Conrad Burns*   1 8 0

Carrot Cake ★ *Senator Carl Levin*   1 8 2

Tom Daschle's Famous Cheesecake ★ *Senator Tom Daschle*   1 8 3

Italian Cream Cake ★ *Representative John T. Myers*   1 8 4

Light Strawberry Cake ★ *Senator Robert F. Bennett*   1 8 6

Fresh Apple Cake ★ *Representative John Tanner*   1 8 7

Cream Cheese Pound Cake ★ *Representative John Tanner*   1 8 8

Nannie's Molasses Cake ★ *Representative Bill Baker*   1 8 9

Lemon Cake ★ *Representative Doug Bereuter*   1 9 0

Lemon Jell-O Cake ★ *Senator Russell Feingold*   1 9 1

Muskingum Chocolate Dew Cake ★ *Senator John Glenn*   1 9 2

Lemon Flip Cake ★ *Senator Richard Lugar*   1 9 3

Apple Cake with Caramel Icing ★ *Representative Tim Hutchinson*   1 9 4

Pies

Key Lime Yogurt Pie ★ *Senator Connie Mack*   1 9 5

New Mexico Apple Pie ★ *Representative Joe Skeen*   1 9 7

Parfait Pie ★ *Representative James B. Longley, Jr.*   1 9 8

Melba Glock's Peach Pie ★ *Senator J. Robert Kerrey*   1 9 9

Chess Pie ★ *Representative John Tanner*   2 0 1

Ice Box Pie ★ *Senator Nancy Landon Kassebaum*   2 0 2

Key Lime Pie ★ *Representative Porter Goss*   2 0 3

Lemon Blossom Chiffon Pie ★ *Representative Nancy L. Johnson*   2 0 4

South Carolina Pecan Pie ★ *Senator Strom Thurmond*   2 0 5

Chocolate Chess Pie ★ *Senator Jesse Helms*   2 0 6

Georgia Pecan Pie ★ *Senator Sam Nunn*   2 0 7

Chocolate Chip Pie ★ *Senator Byron Dorgan*   2 0 8

My Favorite Black Raspberry Pie ★ *Senator Mike DeWine*   2 0 9

Connecticut Yankee Strawberry-Rhubarb Pie ★

Senator Christopher J. Dodd   2 1 0

Cookies

Snicker Doodle Cookies ★ *Senator Dale Bumpers*   2 1 2

John Warner's Favorite Cookies ★ *Senator John Warner*   2 1 3

Maple-Oatmeal Cookies ★ *Senator Judd Gregg*   2 1 4

Grandmother Robb's Oatmeal Cookies ★ *Senator Charles S. Robb*   2 1 5

Grandmother Merrick's Soft Molasses Cookies ★ *Senator William Cohen*   2 1 6

Other Sweets

Texas Brownies ★ *Representative Barbara Cubin*   2 1 7

Double Chocolate Brownies ★ *Senator Sam Nunn*   2 1 9

Light Brownie Pudding ★ *Senator Robert F. Bennett*   2 2 0

French Mint ★ *Senator Orrin Hatch*   2 2 1

Hungarian Rhapsody Dessert ★ *Representative Tom Lantos*   2 2 2

Cousin Susie's Perfect Fudge ★ *Senator Kay Bailey Hutchison*   2 2 3

Ray Hutchison's Homemade Vanilla Ice Cream ★
Senator Kay Bailey Hutchison   2 2 4

Index   225

xvi

★

Contents

Preface

We all have memories that make us smile. A pipe scent may bring memories of your grandfather sitting quietly in his rocking chair, or colored lights may remind you of the electrical reflector turning in a colored circle, gleaming off the shiny red and green glass ornaments, making that aluminum Christmas tree seem like the most beautiful thing you ever saw. There are also those aromas emanating from the kitchen which evoke long-forgotten evenings of laughter, eating Christmas Tortière,* playing cards till after midnight, or just being with the ones that you love.

In this cookbook, I hope to bring back some of those memories for you, to remind you how secure you felt in your mother's cozy kitchen, whether it was in the middle of a large metropolitan city or in a log home on a country lane.

We Americans are fortunate to be able to have all that we have, creating new traditions for our own families, as well as keeping those of the past. So take your children to a new place today, away from the television and video games, by baking up a batch of cookies. Create new memories and traditions with them.

The contributors to *Capitol Cuisine,* current and former leaders of our country, wish for you to take a few of their happy memories in the form of these recipes and make them your own. *Bon appetit!*

*The recipe for Christmas Tortière is on page 57.

Acknowledgments

From the beginning to the end of this project, many people from many states have been a tremendous help to me. I would like to thank Barbara Bush for being the first person to send in a recipe. She gave me encouragement to proceed. Thanks also to Tipper Gore, Nancy Reagan, Rosalynn Carter, Betty Ford, Lady Bird Johnson, Marilyn Quayle, Joan Mondale, and Judy Agnew—without these ladies, this project could not have gone forward.

Next, I would like to thank all of the senators and representatives who took time to respond to my request for a favorite family recipe. This project is really about them, who they are on a personal level. The stories and recipes sent in were delightful to read and delicious to taste.

A special thank you goes to all of my family and friends from around the country who helped me to test these recipes—in Massachusetts: my son, Jesse Milliken, Bonnie Brace, Sharon Mack, Janet Milliken, Marsha Artig, Nancy Petrocelli, and Clark Milliken; in Maine: Constance Borduas, Steven and Shelley Richard, Joan MacDonald, Kelly Beaulieu, Ashley MacDonald, Sue Dollmatsch, Georgie Blais, Betty Bilodeau, and Doris Labreque; in New Hampshire: Kathleen Simoneau; in Connecticut: Wanda Finney and Beth Vadakin; in Florida: Cheryl and Larry Richard, Marie Goldstein, Christal Gibson, and Fran Vivian; in California: Michael and Bonnie Richard, Patricia Perry, and Danielle Miles. Thank you, thank you, thank you!

Thank you also to W. W. Norton for taking a chance on me, for seeing the potential in the cookbook. To Edwin Barber, my editor, who treated me like family, and to Omar Divina, for fielding my many phone calls and answering all of my questions with patience and kindness. To all the other people of W. W. Norton who put the book together in a tasteful manner suitable to the recipe contributors.

Last and most, thank you Rich, for seeing the vision and supporting me emotionally and financially while this project was under way. I love you!

—Diane Milliken
May 1996

xx

★

Acknowledgments

Presidential and Vice-Presidential Dishes

★★★★★★ Hillary Clinton's Chocolate Chips ★★★★★★

By Hillary Clinton

YIELDS 7½ DOZEN COOKIES

3

★

Hillary Clinton

Hillary Rodham Clinton is the wife of President Bill Clinton, the 42nd President of the United States.

INGREDIENTS

Vegetable oil for baking sheets
1½ cups unsifted all-purpose flour
1 teaspoon salt
1 teaspoon baking soda
1 cup solid vegetable shortening
1 cup firmly packed light brown sugar

½ cup granulated sugar
1 teaspoon vanilla
2 eggs
2 cups old-fashioned rolled oats
1 12-ounce package of semi-sweet
  chocolate chips

1. Preheat oven to 350°. Grease baking sheets.
2. Combine flour, salt, and baking soda on waxed paper.
3. Beat together shortening, sugars, and vanilla in large bowl with an electric mixer until creamy. Add eggs, beating until light and fluffy. Gradually beat in flour mixture and rolled oats. Stir in chocolate chips.
4. Drop batter by well-rounded teaspoonfuls onto baking sheet. Bake for 8–10 minutes or until golden.
5. Cool cookies on sheets for 2 minutes. Remove to wire rack to cool completely.

4
★

Presidential and

Vice-Presidential

Dishes

★★★★★★★★★★★★ **Tennessee Treats** ★★★★★★★★★★★★

Submitted by Tipper Gore

SERVES 10—12

66 *I am pleased to send a copy of the Gore family recipe for Tennessee Treats. This recipe is one of my favorites. I hope you will enjoy it too.* Bon appetit!"

—*Tipper Gore is the wife of Vice-President Al Gore, who serves under President Bill Clinton.*

INGREDIENTS

2 cups firmly packed dark brown sugar

2 whole eggs plus 2 egg whites

2 tablespoons honey

1 teaspoon baking powder dissolved in
   ¼ cup boiling water

2 cups flour

⅛ teaspoon allspice

⅛ teaspoon ground cloves

½ teaspoon cinnamon

½ teaspoon salt

½ cup raisins

½ cup chopped dates

½ cup walnut pieces

1. Preheat oven to 350°.

2. In a large mixing bowl, mix brown sugar and eggs. Add honey and stir. Add baking powder and water mixture and stir.

3. Combine flour and spices and stir into mixture.

4. Add remaining ingredients and stir.

5. Pour into greased 8-inch baking pan.

6. Bake for 30–40 minutes. To determine when treats are ready, insert a toothpick—a nearly dry toothpick indicates they are done.

7. Cut into squares while warm.

Submitted by Barbara Bush

5
★

Barbara Bush

SERVES 4   MAKES APPROXIMATELY 6 CUPS SAUCE

❝*T*❞*his dish is a favorite of the Bushes, and Barbara Bush hopes that you will enjoy it too!"*
—*Barbara Bush is the wife of former President George Bush, the 41st President of the United States, who served from 1989 to 1993 as President, and from 1981 to 1989 as Vice-President under President Ronald Reagan.*

Preparation Tip: This recipe can be grilled on coals or baked in the oven. Delicious either way!

CHICKEN MARINADE INGREDIENTS

1 3-pound chicken fryer, quartered
1 large clove garlic, crushed
1 teaspoon salt
½ teaspoon freshly ground pepper
1 tablespoon oil
3 tablespoons lemon juice

HOMEMADE BARBECUE SAUCE

¼ cup cider vinegar
2¼ cups water
¾ cup sugar
1 stick butter or margarine
⅓ cup yellow mustard
2 onions, coarsely chopped
½ teaspoon each salt and pepper
½ cup Worcestershire sauce
2½ cups ketchup
6–8 tablespoons lemon juice
Cayenne pepper to taste

1. Put marinade ingredients in a heavy zippered storage bag. Shake to coat well. Refrigerate 24 hours if possible, turning the bag several times.

2. If grilling, when coals are ready, place chicken on the grill, skin side up, and baste with the marinade. Cook until well browned before turning—approximately 15–25 minutes on each side.

3. If baking in oven, preheat oven to 400° and bake skin side down first.

4. About 20 minutes before chicken is done, begin using your favorite bottled barbecue sauce or the homemade version (below).

Barbecue Sauce:

1. Bring vinegar, water, sugar, butter, mustard, onions, salt and pepper to a boil. Cook on low 20 minutes, or until onion is tender.

2. Then add Worcestershire sauce, ketchup, lemon juice, and cayenne pepper.

3. Simmer slowly for 45 minutes. Taste for seasonings.

This homemade barbecue sauce freezes well.

6

Presidential and Vice-Presidential Dishes

★★★★★★★ **Red, White, and Blue Cobbler** ★★★★★★★

Submitted by Barbara Bush

7
★

Barbara Bush

SERVES 6

*B*arbara Bush is the wife of former President George Bush, the 41st President of the United States, who served from 1989 to 1993 as President, and from 1981 to 1989 as Vice-President under President Ronald Reagan.

Preparation Tip: The cobbler can be made with canned pie filling or with the homemade version in the recipe, depending on how much time you have. Use either for great results. Serve hot, topped with vanilla ice cream.

INGREDIENTS

Blueberry Filling:

1 21-ounce can blueberry filling

Or:

¼ cup sugar

½ tablespoon cornstarch

½ teaspoon lemon juice

2 cups fresh or frozen unsweetened
    blueberries

Cherry Filling:

1 21-ounce can cherry filling

Or:

½ cup plus 2 tablespoons sugar

1½ tablespoons cornstarch

1 21-ounce can sour cherries and their
juice

⅛ teaspoon almond extract

⅛ teaspoon cinnamon

Topping:

1 cup flour

1 tablespoon sugar

1½ teaspoons baking powder

½ teaspoon salt

3 tablespoons shortening

½ cup milk

Blueberry Filling

1. Mix sugar and cornstarch in a saucepan and add lemon juice and blueberries. Cook until thickened.

2. Put into an 8 x 8 Pyrex dish and keep hot in a 250° oven while making cherry filling.

Cherry Filling

1. Mix sugar and cornstarch in a saucepan. Gradually stir in juice from canned cherries and cook until thickened, adding cherries, almond extract, and cinnamon at the end.

2. Smooth cherry filling over blueberry mixture. Keep hot while making topping.

Topping

1. Turn oven up to 400°.

2. Mix dry ingredients and shortening until mixture is like fine crumbs.

3. Stir in milk and drop by spoonfuls onto hot filling.

4. Bake for 25–30 minutes, or until golden brown.

★★★★★★★★★★★★★★★★ Cole Slaw ★★★★★★★★★★★★★★★★

Submitted by Barbara Bush

SERVES 8–10

*B*arbara Bush is the wife of former President George Bush, the 41st President of the United States, who served from 1989 to 1993 as President, and from 1981 to 1989 as Vice-President under President Ronald Reagan.

INGREDIENTS

2 medium heads cabbage, finely shredded
   (may add some purple cabbage for
   color)
Salt
2 medium white or purple onions, chopped
4 green onions, finely sliced
2 teaspoons salt

⅓ cup sugar
1 teaspoon dry mustard
½ cup cider vinegar
¾ cup vegetable oil
Freshly ground black pepper to taste
4 heaping tablespoons light or nonfat
   mayonnaise

1. Sprinkle cabbage with salt and let drain in a colander about 2 hours, squeezing as much water out as possible before continuing. May drain overnight if desired.

2. Transfer cabbage to a large bowl. Add onions.

3. In a small bowl, mix remaining ingredients and stir into cabbage mixture.

4. Adjust seasonings if needed by adding a bit more sugar first, and if necessary, more salt.

5. Cover and refrigerate until ready to serve.

9
★
Barbara Bush

★★★★★★★★★★★★ Monkey Bread ★★★★★★★★★★★★★

Submitted by Nancy Reagan

MAKES 2 LOAVES   SERVES 6–8 EACH LOAF

*N*ancy Reagan is the wife of former President Ronald Reagan, the 40th President of the United States, who served from 1981 to 1989.

INGREDIENTS

¾ ounce yeast or 1 package dry yeast

1–1¼ cups milk, heated to lukewarm

3 eggs

3 tablespoons sugar

1 teaspoon salt

3½ cups flour

6 ounces butter, at room temperature

½ pound melted butter

1. Butter and flour 2 9-inch ring molds.

2. In a large bowl, mix yeast with part of milk until dissolved.

3. Add 2 eggs, and beat.

4. Mix in dry ingredients.

5. Add remaining milk a little at a time, mixing thoroughly.

6. Cut in butter until blended.

7. Knead dough, then let rise 1–1½ hours, until double in size.

8. Knead again, and let rise 40 minutes.

9. Roll dough onto floured board; shape into a log. Cut log into 28 pieces of equal size. Shape each piece of dough into a ball and roll in melted butter.

10. Use half the balls in each ring mold. Place 7 balls on the bottom of each mold, leaving space between. Place remaining balls on top, spacing evenly. Let dough rise in mold.

11. While dough is rising, preheat oven to 375°.

12. Beat remaining egg and brush tops of loaves with it.

13. Bake until golden brown, approximately 15 minutes.

★★★ Cream of Broccoli Soup, with No Cream ★★★

Submitted by Rosalynn Carter

ll

★

Rosalynn Carter

SERVES 4

"*This is a great low-fat recipe for those watching calories or cholesterol.*"
—*Rosalynn Carter is the wife of former President Jimmy Carter, the 39th President of the United States, who served from 1977 to 1981.*

Preparation Tip: If you are watching calories, fat, and cholesterol, use low-fat or fat-free plain yogurt in place of the sour cream. There are now even fat-free sour creams on the market that would be great in this recipe.

INGREDIENTS

1 medium onion, chopped
1 clove garlic, crushed
1 tablespoon sunflower oil, or other
*   vegetable oil*
1 bay leaf
1 pound green broccoli, chopped
1 small potato (for thickening)

2½ cups light vegetable stock (or broth
*   made with vegetables, or chicken*
*   bouillon)*
Salt and pepper
Juice of ½ lemon
Sour cream

1. Sauté onion and garlic in the oil with bay leaf until soft, or in saucepan sprayed with nonstick cooking spray, 3–4 minutes.

2. Add broccoli, potato, and stock and simmer gently, covered, for about 10 minutes, when the broccoli should be tender but still bright green. Remove bay leaf and let cool a little.

3. Puree in a blender (not totally smooth). Season with salt and pepper to taste; add lemon juice. May need reheating in clean pan before serving.

4. Add a dollop of sour cream just before serving.

★

Presidential and

Vice-Presidential

Dishes

★★★★★★★★★★★★ **Blu'Bana Bread** ★★★★★★★★★★★★

Submitted by Betty Ford

MAKES 2 LOAVES   SERVES 6–8 EACH LOAF

66 *This recipe is one that the Ford family has always enjoyed."*
— *Betty Ford is the wife of former President Gerald Ford, the 38th President of the United States, who served from 1974 to 1977, and from 1973 to 1974 as Vice-President under Richard Nixon.*

INGREDIENTS

2 cups sugar

2 sticks butter

4 eggs

2 teaspoons vanilla

5 ripe bananas, mashed

4 cups sifted flour

3 teaspoons allspice

2 teaspoons baking soda

1 teaspoon baking powder

½ teaspoon salt

2 cups fresh or frozen blueberries, drained

1. Preheat oven to 325°.
2. Grease and flour 2 5 x 9 loaf pans.
3. Cream together sugar and butter. Beat in eggs, then add vanilla.
4. Fold in mashed bananas and 2 cups of the flour.
5. Place 2 remaining cups of flour, less 2 tablespoons, in sifter and add allspice, baking soda, baking powder, and salt. Sift and fold into batter.
6. Sprinkle blueberries with remaining flour, coat well, and fold into the batter.
7. Divide batter into loaf pans; bake for approximately 50 minutes.
8. Test with toothpick—bread is done if toothpick comes out dry.

★★★★★★★★★ Shrimp-Squash Casserole ★★★★★★★★★

Submitted by Lady Bird Johnson

SERVES 4–6

*L*ady Bird Johnson is the wife of former President Lyndon B. Johnson, the 36th President of the United States, who served from 1963 to 1969, and as Vice-President under President John F. Kennedy from 1961 to 1963.

Lady Bird Johnson

INGREDIENTS

Yellow squash, washed, dried, and
   cut crosswise into ¼-inch slices to
   make 3 cups
2 tablespoons margarine
2 tablespoons flour
½ teaspoon salt
⅛ teaspoon pepper
1 cup chicken broth

½ cup whipping cream
1 tablespoon finely minced onion
¾ cup raw shrimp, rinsed in cold water,
   drained, and shelled
½ cup coarse bread crumbs
¼ cup grated Parmesan cheese
1 tablespoon melted margarine

1. Preheat oven to 400°.

2. Heat margarine in saucepan. Blend in flour, salt, and pepper. Cook until it bubbles.

3. Remove from heat and add chicken broth gradually, stirring constantly. Bring to a boil and boil for 1–2 minutes.

4. Blend in cream and minced onion.

5. Mix in raw shrimp.

6. Layer half the squash in a 1½-quart casserole dish. Spoon half the shrimp sauce over squash. Repeat with remaining squash and shrimp sauce. Cover tightly and bake for 30 minutes.

7. Meanwhile, toss crumbs and Parmesan cheese with melted margarine. After 30 minutes, top squash with bread crumb mixture.

8. Reduce oven heat to 350° and return casserole to oven for 15 minutes, or until crumbs are golden brown.

★★★★★★★★★★★★ **Peach Cobbler** ★★★★★★★★★★★★★

Submitted by Marilyn Quayle

SERVES 6–8

❝One of the Quayles' favorite recipes.**❞**
—*Marilyn Quayle is the wife of former Vice-President Daniel Quayle, who served under President George Bush from 1989 to 1993.*

INGREDIENTS

Peach Filling:

⅓–⅔ cups sugar
1 tablespoon cornstarch
¼ cup water
4 cups fresh or frozen peach slices or
    unsweetened canned peach slices,
    drained

Topping:

1 cup all-purpose flour
¼ cup sugar
1 teaspoon baking powder
½ teaspoon ground cinnamon (optional)
3 tablespoons margarine or butter
1 egg, beaten
3 tablespoons milk

1. Preheat oven to 400°.

2. Prepare filling. In a saucepan, combine sugar and cornstarch. Add water and stir in peaches. Cook and stir till thickened and bubbly. Keep hot.

3. Mix flour, sugar, baking powder, and cinnamon. Cut in margarine until mixture resembles coarse crumbs.

4. Combine egg and milk. Add to flour mixture, stirring just to moisten.

5. Transfer hot filling to an 8 x 8 x 2 baking dish. Drop topping in 6 mounds atop filling.

6. Bake 20–25 minutes, or until a toothpick inserted into topping comes out clean.

★★★★★★★★★★★★ **Salted Nut Bars** ★★★★★★★★★★★★

Submitted by Joan Mondale
From the Kitchen of Lynda Pedersen

SERVES 8–10

66 *H*ere *is a recipe I use for bars to be served to our guests in the Ambassa-dor's residence in Tokyo. I wanted to serve something very American, along with Japanese treats."*

—*Joan Mondale is the wife of former Vice-President Walter Mondale, who served under President Jimmy Carter from 1977 to 1981. Walter Mondale is currently Ambassador to Japan.*

15
★
Joan Mondale

INGREDIENTS

1½ cups flour
¾ cup brown sugar
½ teaspoon salt
½ cup butter
1 cup butterscotch chips

½ cup white corn syrup
2 tablespoons butter
1 teaspoon vanilla
1 12-ounce can mixed nuts

1. Preheat oven to 350°.
2. Mix flour, brown sugar, salt, and ½ cup butter with pastry blender or fork.
3. Pat into a 9 x 13 pan and bake 10 minutes.
4. Melt together butterscotch chips, corn syrup, 2 tablespoons butter, and vanilla; then add nuts.
5. Pour over crust and bake an additional 10 minutes.

★★★★★★★★★★★ **Spaghetti Sauce** ★★★★★★★★★★★

Submitted by Judy Agnew

SERVES 4–6

*J*udy Agnew is the wife of former Vice-President Spiro T. Agnew, who served under President Richard M. Nixon from 1969 to 1973.

Preparation Tip: This spaghetti sauce will be great with any of your favorite pastas.

INGREDIENTS

1 pound ground beef
⅛ teaspoon pepper
1 small onion, chopped
1 tablespoon Worcestershire sauce

½ green pepper, chopped
¼ teaspoon dried oregano
1 26-ounce can tomato sauce

1. Cook ground beef, crumbling meat as it cooks. Drain.
2. In a separate pan, mix remaining ingredients and heat thoroughly. Stir in beef.

★★★★★★★★★★ **Grape Juice Fruit Ice** ★★★★★★★★★★

Submitted by Judy Agnew

SERVES 10–12

*J*udy Agnew is the wife of former Vice-President Spiro T. Agnew, who served under President Richard M. Nixon from 1969 to 1973.

Preparation Tip: When we were preparing this recipe, my son Jesse came up with the suggestion of pouring the mixture into ice cube trays and adding toothpicks to make pops for the kids. It worked out great!

17
★

Judy Agnew

INGREDIENTS

1 cup water
¼ teaspoon salt
1 cup sugar
2 cups grape juice

1 cup orange juice
¼ cup pineapple juice
¼ cup lemon juice

1. Put water, salt, and sugar in saucepan and bring to a boil.

2. Remove from heat and, when cool, combine with juices. Pour into freezer pan and put in freezer. It will take about 4 hours to freeze.

3. After 1½ hours, stir.

Beef Dishes

✶✶✶✶✶✶✶✶✶ **Lite and Lean Beef Broil** ✶✶✶✶✶✶✶✶✶✶

Submitted by Senator Larry E. Craig
From the Kitchen of Suzanne Craig

✶

Larry E. Craig

SERVES 4–6

❝ *This dish was served on July 8, 1983, at the wedding luncheon of Suzanne and Larry Craig in Midvale, Idaho.*❞
—*Senator Larry E. Craig is a Republican and represents the state of Idaho.*

INGREDIENTS
1½ pounds beef sirloin steak, top round, flank, or brisket
Sesame seeds

Marinade:
½ cup soy sauce
¼ cup water
2 tablespoons lemon juice
2 tablespoons honey
1 teaspoon instant minced onion
¼ teaspoon garlic powder

1. Combine marinade ingredients in a nonmetal pan.
2. Add beef and turn to coat. Marinate beef for 24–48 hours in refrigerator.
3. Broil beef to desired doneness (do not overcook; best served medium rare).
4. Slice beef across the grain into thin slices.
5. Sprinkle with sesame seeds.

★★★★★★★★★★★★★ Wild Rice Stew ★★★★★★★★★★★★★

Submitted by Senator Bob Packwood

SERVES 4–6

*F*ormer Senator Bob Packwood is a Republican from the state of Oregon.

INGREDIENTS

1½ pounds good beef stew meat, cut into chunks
Red wine for marinade (optional)
1 package Uncle Ben's Long Grain and Wild Rice, including seasonings

1 10¼-ounce can onion soup, undiluted
1 10¾-ounce can mushroom soup, undiluted

1. Preheat oven to 325°.
2. Marinate meat in wine if desired.
3. Mix all ingredients except wine in casserole dish.
4. Bake covered for approximately 2 hours.

★★★★★★★★★★ **Dakota Bean Salad** ★★★★★★★★★★

Submitted by Senator Larry Pressler
From the Kitchen of Harriet Pressler

Larry Pressler

SERVES 10–15

*S*enator Larry E. Pressler is a Republican and represents the state of South Dakota.

Preparation Tip: This recipe makes a large quantity of bean salad, so it would be great for a Super Bowl party, or any event where you may have a large group of people. You may cut this recipe down for smaller portions. Use your favorite dressing—Italian, Caesar, or vinaigrette. The light versions of these dressings served on the side will keep this recipe healthy and low in fat.

INGREDIENTS

2½ pounds pork or beef tenderloins

1 15-ounce can each pinto, white, black, garbanzo, red and pink kidney, and fava beans

1 cup celery hearts, sliced

1 red onion, cut in rings

1 large clove garlic, crushed

½ cup each green, yellow, and red peppers, diced

½ cup each yellow and white corn, fresh or frozen

½ cup sliced raw carrots

2 cups cooked brown rice

1. Bake tenderloins to desired doneness, 5–10 minutes. Chill completely. Cube into bite-size pieces.

2. Blanch corn and drain.

3. In a very large bowl, toss together rinsed and drained beans, celery, onion, garlic, peppers, corn, and carrots. Fold in cooked rice and meat.

4. Add your favorite dressing to taste.

5. Serve cold with your favorite bread.

★★★★★★★★★★ **Dakota Bean Stew** ★★★★★★★★★★★

Submitted by Senator Larry Pressler
From the Kitchen of Harriet Pressler

SERVES 10–15   MAKES APPROXIMATELY 1 GALLON STEW

"*This colorful Dakota Bean Stew goes well with your favorite salad and bread.*"
—*Senator Larry E. Pressler is a Republican and represents the state of South Dakota.*

INGREDIENTS

1 12–14 ounce package mixed-variety dried beans (select package with 5 or more varieties)
⅓ cup flour
Salt and pepper to taste
1½ pounds beef or pork tenderloins, cut into chunks
¼ cup olive oil
1 cup celery hearts, finely diced
1 cup red onion, finely diced

3 large cloves garlic, crushed
8 cups water
2 10¼-ounce cans beef consommé
½ cup each green, yellow, and red pepper, diced
½ cup each white and yellow corn, fresh or frozen
½ cup sliced carrots, fresh or frozen
2 cups cooked brown rice

1. Rinse and soak beans according to package directions.

2. Put flour and salt and pepper to taste in brown paper bag. Add cut-up meat. Shake well.

3. Brown coated meat in olive oil in large Dutch oven.

4. Add celery and red onion, cooking for 2 minutes. Add garlic and continue cooking until vegetables are soft.

5. Add water and consommé to mixture; bring to boil. Add beans and simmer until beans are tender, about 3 hours, adding more water if needed.

6. Add peppers, corn, and carrots. Simmer an additional ½ hour.

7. Fold in rice. Heat through.

Freezes well.

★★★★★★★★ **Keftedes (Greek Meatballs)** ★★★★★★★★

Submitted by Representative Michael Bilirakis

SERVES 4–6

Congressman Michael Bilirakis is a Republican and represents the 9th District of Florida.

Preparation Tip: This dish may be served as an appetizer or as a main dish.

INGREDIENTS

1 pound ground beef
1 onion, chopped
2 fresh tomatoes, chopped, or 1 14½-
    ounce can whole tomatoes, drained and
    chopped
1 clove garlic, chopped

Salt and pepper to taste
Juice of 1 lemon
1 egg
1 cup flour
Corn oil

1. Mix all ingredients except flour and oil. Form the mixture into meatballs.
2. Roll meatballs in flour and fry in oil in a nonstick frying pan.

25
★

Michael Bilirakis

★★★★★★★ **Marinated Eye of the Round** ★★★★★★★

Submitted by Representative Charlie Rose

SERVES 10–15

66 *D elicious for a buffet supper."*
—*Congressman Charlie Rose is a Democrat and represent the 7th District of North Carolina.*

INGREDIENTS

1 5-pound eye-of-the-round roast
¼ cup salad oil
½ cup vinegar
½ cup lemon juice

½ cup soy sauce
½ cup Worcestershire sauce
½ teaspoon black pepper

1. Marinate roast in a Pyrex dish for 24 hours in refrigerator, turning over several times to cover all surfaces.
2. Preheat oven to 250°.
3. Cook, uncovered, in the marinade for 2½ hours.
4. Refrigerate overnight.
5. Slice thin and serve with heated marinade.

Freezes well.

★★★★★★★★ South Dakota Taco Salad ★★★★★★★★★

Submitted by Senator Tom Daschle

SERVES 6–8

27
★

Tom Daschle

66 *Makes a main meal on a hot day, as this is really a beef dish and a salad in one. This is a real South Dakota tradition on the plains."*
—*Senator Tom Daschle is a Democrat and represents the state of South Dakota.*

INGREDIENTS

1 pound ground beef
1 1½-ounce package taco seasoning mix
1 head lettuce, chopped or torn
Sliced tomatoes
1 green pepper, diced (optional)
1 15-ounce can red kidney beans, drained

8 ounces shredded cheddar cheese
1 10-ounce bottle Russian dressing, or
    Thousand Island dressing
8 taco shells or crushed taco-flavored
    chips, such as Doritos

1. Brown meat. Drain. Add taco seasoning mix according to directions. Cool beef after adding seasoning.

2. Cut up lettuce, tomatoes, and pepper as you would for a garden salad.

3. Mix all with cooled beef, beans, and cheese.

4. Carefully mix in dressing.

5. When ready to serve, crush taco shells and carefully fold into the salad for a nice crunchy taste.

✮✮✮✮✮✮✮✮✮✮ Swedish Meatballs ✮✮✮✮✮✮✮✮✮✮

Submitted by Representative Charles Stenholm
From the Kitchen of Cindy Stenholm

MAKES APPROXIMATELY 3 DOZEN

Congressman Charles Stenholm is a Democrat and represents the 17th District of Texas.

INGREDIENTS

1¼ pounds ground beef
¼ pound ground pork
1½ cups soft bread crumbs (about 3 slices bread)
1 cup light cream or half-and-half
½ cup chopped onion
3 tablespoons butter or margarine
1 egg

¼ teaspoon ginger
Dash of nutmeg
Salt and pepper to taste
3 tablespoons flour
¾ cup canned condensed beef broth
¼ cup water
¼ teaspoon instant coffee

1. Mix meats together.
2. Soak bread crumbs in cream about 5 minutes.
3. Cook onion in 1 tablespoon of the butter until tender.
4. Combine meat, crumb mixture, onion, egg, and seasonings. Beat vigorously with electric mixer until fluffy.
5. Form into 1½-inch balls (mixture will be soft). Brown in the remaining 2 tablespoons butter, shaking skillet to keep balls round. Remove meatballs.
6. Stir flour into drippings in skillet; add broth, water, and coffee. Heat and stir until gravy thickens. Return meatballs to gravy. Cover and cook slowly about 30 minutes, basting occasionally.

May be frozen.

★★★★★★★★ "Bohemian" Teriyaki Beef ★★★★★★★★

Submitted by Senator J. James Exon
From the Kitchen of Mrs. J. J. Exon

SERVES 6–8

66 *This is Mrs. J. James Exon's first-place winning recipe from the 1990 Nebraska State Fair Celebrity Cook-Off."*
—*Senator J. James Exon is a Democrat and represents the state of Nebraska.*

29
★

J. James Exon

INGREDIENTS
2 pounds top sirloin, cut 1 inch thick
Plum jelly

Marinade:
½ cup soy sauce
¼ cup brown sugar
2 tablespoons olive oil
2 tablespoons plum jelly
1 teaspoon dry ginger
¼ teaspoon lemon pepper
¼ teaspoon garlic salt

1. Combine marinade ingredients.
2. Cut sirloin in ¼-inch strips and marinate, in refrigerator, for 2 hours.
3. Place meat, accordion style, on skewers over hot grill.
4. Keep turning meat and brush with marinade until done, approximately 8–10 minutes.
5. Serve with plum jelly as a condiment.

★★★★★★ **Exon Family Favorite Casserole** ★★★★★★

Submitted by Senator J. James Exon
From the Kitchen of Mrs. J. James Exon

SERVES 8–10

Senator J. James Exon is a Democrat and represents the state of Nebraska.

INGREDIENTS

1½ pounds ground beef
½ cup chopped onion
2 8-ounce cans tomato sauce
1 teaspoon sugar
1 teaspoon salt
¼ teaspoon garlic salt
¼ teaspoon pepper

1 cup sour cream
8 ounces cream cheese
⅓ cup chopped green onion
¼ cup chopped green pepper
3 cups cooked noodles
Velveeta cheese (shredded)

1. Preheat oven to 350°.
2. In a large skillet, cook meat and onion until meat is lightly brown and onion is tender.
3. Stir in tomato sauce, sugar, salt, garlic salt, and pepper. Remove from heat.
4. Combine sour cream, cream cheese, green onion, and green pepper.
5. Cook noodles according to package directions and drain. Spread half the noodles in a baking dish, top with meat mixture, and cover with sour cream mixture. Add remaining noodles and meat sauce.
6. Top with Velveeta cheese.
7. Bake for 30 minutes.

Poultry Dishes

★★★★★★★★★★ **Oriental Chicken Salad** ★★★★★★★★★★

Submitted by Senator David Pryor

SERVES 6

66 *D*ue to the fact that I now must maintain a healthier diet, as I urge everyone to do, I am enclosing a recipe for Oriental Chicken Salad." —*Senator David Pryor is a Democrat and represents the state of Arkansas.*

INGREDIENTS
1 large breast of roasting chicken (about 5 pounds)

Salad:
3 bunches watercress, chopped
1 bunch green onions, sliced
1 8-ounce can water chestnuts, sliced
6 ounces bean sprouts, fresh if possible
3 stalks celery, sliced
1 large head romaine lettuce, chopped

Garnish (divide among 6 dishes):
12 cucumber slices
6 ounces julienne carrot
6 large fresh mushrooms, sliced
6 radish roses

Dressing:
6 ounces olive oil
6 ounces low-sodium soy sauce
Dash of cinnamon

1. Poach or steam chicken breast until done. (Poaching liquid can be saved for a soup or sauce.) After cooling, bone chicken and shred, using your fingers or a fork.

2. Mix watercress, scallions, water chestnuts, bean sprouts, celery, and half the chicken together. Toss with half the dressing.

3. Place romaine lettuce on six plates or large bowls. Divide salad mixture between plates. Arrange garnishes and remaining chicken on top of salad.

4. Serve remaining dressing on the side.

★★★★★★★★★★★★★★ **Peachy Chicken** ★★★★★★★★★★★★★★

Submitted by Senator Connie Mack

SERVES 6

*T*his recipe is one of Senator Mack's favorites and came from The Good Book of Nutrition.*
—*Senator Connie Mack is a Republican and represents the state of Florida.*

INGREDIENTS
½ cup peach preserves
½ cup water
Juice of ½ lemon
6 chicken breasts, skinned and boned

1. In a small bowl, combine peach preserves, water, and lemon juice; mix well.

2. Arrange chicken in a shallow dish. Pour preserves mixture over chicken.

3. Marinate in refrigerator overnight.

4. Preheat oven to 350°.

5. Drain chicken, reserving marinade.

6. Arrange chicken in a baking dish. Bake for 45 minutes, or until chicken is tender, basting frequently with reserved marinade.

7. Serve with rice.

*Nashville, Tenn.: Great American Opportunities, 1987. Recipe contains approximately per serving: 217 calories; 3.1 grams of fat; 12.85 percent calories from fat. Used with the permission of the American Cancer Society.

J. Bennett Johnston's
★★★★★★★★★★ **Favorite Chicken Salad** ★★★★★★★★★★

Submitted by Senator J. Bennett Johnston

35
★

J. Bennett Johnston

SERVES 6

*S*enator J. Bennett Johnston is a Democrat and represents the state of Louisiana.

Preparation Tip: For large groups, use 3 cans pineapple chunks and double everything else. Especially delicious served with croissants and melon.

INGREDIENTS

3 chicken breasts (6 halves), skinned and boned
1¼ cups water
1 15-ounce can pineapple chunks, drained (save juice)
1½ cups chopped celery (not diced, but chunkier)

1 cup cashews or walnuts
3 large or 4 small Red Delicious apples, peel on, chopped in chunks and dipped in pineapple juice so they don't discolor
Kraft Lemon Mayonnaise, or plain mayonnaise mixed with lemon juice

1. Preheat oven to 350°.

2. Bake chicken in Dutch oven with water for 45–60 minutes. Drain the chicken and cut into chunks.

3. Mix all chunks in large bowl.

4. Just before serving, toss with mayonnaise.

36
★

Poultry Dishes

★★★★★★★★★ **Chicken Caruso and Rice** ★★★★★★★★★

Submitted by Senator John Kerry

SERVES 6

66 *I have enjoyed making this for years, although the amount of time I have to spend dabbling in the culinary arts is limited!"*
—*Senator John Kerry is a Democrat and represents the state of Massachusetts.*

INGREDIENTS

2 whole chicken breasts (about ½ pound) skinned, boned, and cut into thin strips
Garlic salt
Pepper
3 tablespoons butter or margarine

1 30-ounce jar spaghetti sauce (about 2 cups)
1 teaspoon Italian seasoning
2 cups sliced celery
3 cups cooked rice
Grated Parmesan cheese (optional)

1. Season chicken to taste with garlic salt and pepper and sauté in butter or margarine for about 10 minutes.

2. Stir in sauce and Italian seasoning; cover and simmer for 10 minutes.

3. Add celery; continue cooking until celery is tender (or crisp), according to taste.

4. Serve over rice, sprinkled with grated Parmesan cheese, if desired.

★★★★★★★★ Garlic-Chicken Phyllo Rolls ★★★★★★★★

Submitted by Representative Calvin Dooley

SERVES 6

Congressman Calvin Dooley is a Democrat and represents the 20th District of California.

INGREDIENTS

2 heads fresh garlic
½ cup water
½ cup dry white wine
Juice of 1 lemon
¼ teaspoon salt
1 pound boned and skinned chicken
    breasts
6 sheets phyllo dough
¼ cup butter, melted
2½ ounces thinly sliced prosciutto
2 cups grated Swiss cheese

SAUCE

1 large onion, chopped
2 tablespoons butter
1 13-ounce can sliced mushrooms, drained
1 10¾-ounce can cream of mushroom soup
½ cup jelly (any variety)

37
★
Calvin Dooley

1. Preheat oven to 400°.

2. Separate garlic into cloves and drop into boiling water. Simmer 1 minute, drain, peel, and mash lightly with a fork.

3. Bring water, wine, lemon juice, and salt to a simmer in a large saucepan. Add chicken and garlic. Cook at a bare simmer, turning occasionally, until chicken is just cooked, approximately 20 minutes. Remove chicken and continue cooking garlic until tender. Drain.

4. Cut chicken into large chunks and divide into 6 portions.

5. Lay out 1 phyllo sheet, brush half with melted butter and fold in half crosswise. Brush with butter again. Top with a portion of chicken and garlic cloves. Top with ⅙ of the prosciutto and ⅓ cup cheese. Fold in the sides and roll up.

6. Repeat with remaining phyllo sheets. Work quickly so phyllo doesn't dry out.

7. Place rolls on lightly greased baking sheet and brush with butter. Bake about 20 minutes, until golden.

8. Sauté chopped onion in butter until tender. Add remaining sauce ingredients and simmer.

9. To serve, spoon sauce over rolls.

38

★

Poultry Dishes

★★★★★★★★★★ **Chicken Tetrazzini** ★★★★★★★★★★

Submitted by Senator Howell Heflin
From the Kitchen of Mrs. Howell Heflin

SERVES 6–8

66 *This dish is great served with fruit, congealed salad, or green vegetables and rolls.*
—*Senator Howell Heflin is a Democrat and represents the state of Alabama.*

Preparation Tip: Use your favorite chicken broth, whether homemade or store-bought, to cook onions, celery, peppers, and vermicelli in. This will bring the taste of the broth into the vegetables and pasta. The amount of broth needed may vary according to preparation.

INGREDIENTS

1 cup chopped onions
1 cup chopped celery
1 bell pepper, diced
1 8-ounce package vermicelli
8 cups chicken broth
3½ pounds chicken or more, cooked, skinned, boned, and cut into small chunks

1 10-¾-ounce can cream of mushroom soup
1 13½-ounce can cut-up mushrooms, drained
1 4-ounce can chopped pimientos
8 ounces grated sharp cheddar cheese

1. Preheat oven to 350°.
2. Cook onions, celery, pepper, and vermicelli in chicken broth just until pasta is tender. Remove from broth and mix together with all remaining ingredients in a 3-quart casserole dish. If it looks dry, add a little broth.
3. Bake until bubbly, about 30 minutes.

★★★ **Mrs. Sheila Wellstone's Curried Chicken** ★★★

Submitted by Senator Paul David Wellstone
From the Kitchen of Sheila Wellstone

SERVES 6–8

66 *Serve this dish with your favorite rice, chutney, and other condiments such as salted peanuts, flaked coconut, or raisins, and enjoy! I guarantee it is delicious and that it will become one of your favorites too!"*
—*Senator Paul David Wellstone is a Democrat and represents the state of Minnesota.*

INGREDIENTS

6–8 whole chicken breasts, halved, boned, and skinned (wash and dry)
4 tablespoons butter or oil
2 small onions
1 clove garlic
2 tablespoons flour
2 tablespoons curry powder

2 teaspoons ground ginger
2 teaspoons cardamom
1 teaspoon salt
1 14-ounce can whole tomatoes, drained and chopped
1 cup peeled and chopped apples
2 cups chicken broth

1. Brown chicken in butter or oil. Remove chicken from pan.

2. Sauté onions and garlic in same pan. Combine flour, curry powder, ground ginger, cardamom, and salt. Add to onions and stir.

3. Add tomatoes, apples, and chicken broth. Stir well and simmer 5 minutes.

4. Add chicken and simmer until chicken is tender, 15–20 minutes.

Grilled Pesto-Stuffed Chicken
with Lemon Butter

★★★★★★★★★★★ ★★★★★★★★★★★★

Submitted by Representative Bill Archer

SERVES 4

Congressman Bill Archer is a Republican and represents the 7th District of Texas.

INGREDIENTS

4 chicken breast halves, bones and skin
   intact

4 tablespoons thick pesto sauce

4 tablespoons unsalted butter

2 tablespoons freshly squeezed lemon juice

1. Run fingers between skin and flesh of each breast to make a pocket, being careful not to tear or remove skin. Stuff 1 tablespoon pesto into each pocket. Secure with toothpicks if necessary.

2. Heat butter and lemon juice in small saucepan until butter melts.

3. Place chicken breasts on a grill over medium-hot coals and cook 30–40 minutes, turning and basting with lemon butter every 10 minutes.

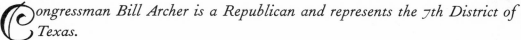

41
★

Bill Archer

★★★★★★★★★★ **Chicken Breast Dinner** ★★★★★★★★★★★

Submitted by Senator Paul D. Coverdell

SERVES 6–8

$\mathcal{S}$enator Paul D. Coverdell is a Republican and represents the state of Georgia.

INGREDIENTS

8 chicken breasts (skinned and boned)

8 slices bacon

1 5-ounce jar dried beef, cut into small squares

1 10-¾-ounce can cream of mushroom soup

¾ cup milk

1 16-ounce container sour cream

1. Preheat oven to 350°.

2. Butter the bottom of a rectangular baking dish.

3. Roll chicken breasts up and wrap a slice of bacon around each. Then lay them in dish.

4. Mix mushroom soup, milk, and about ¾ of the sour cream (12 ounces) over low heat. Stir about ¾ of the dried beef into mixture.

5. Pour this mixture over chicken and bake about 2 hours.

6. Sprinkle with remaining beef and bake an additional 10 minutes.

7. Spread remaining 4 ounces of sour cream over the top.

★★★★★ Sweet and Sour Chicken (Low-Fat) ★★★★★

Submitted by Senator Robert F. Bennett

Robert F. Bennett

SERVES 6–8

*S*enator Robert F. Bennett is a Republican and represents the state of Utah.

INGREDIENTS

1½ pounds skinned and boned chicken
   breasts, cut in strips
½ cup water
1 20-ounce can pineapple chunks,
   drained, juice reserved
¼ cup brown sugar
2 tablespoons cornstarch

¼ cup vinegar
1 tablespoon soy sauce
½ teaspoon salt
1 small green pepper, cut in strips
1 small red pepper, cut in strips
¼ cup sliced green onions

1. Brown chicken in hot skillet sprayed with nonstick cooking spray; add water. Cover and simmer until done, about 10 minutes. Set aside.

2. Combine pineapple juice, brown sugar, cornstarch, vinegar, soy sauce, and salt in a saucepan; cook and stir over medium heat until thick. Pour over hot chicken and let stand for 10 minutes. (Or, refrigerate at this point and complete preparation when ready to serve. Reheat chicken mixture before continuing.)

3. Add green and red peppers, green onion, and pineapple. Cook 2–3 minutes.

4. Serve over rice.

★★★★★★★★★★★★ **Chicken Scallopini** ★★★★★★★★★★★★

Submitted by Senator Alfonse D'Amato
From the Kitchen of Antoinette D'Amato

SERVES 3

*S*enator Alfonse D'Amato is a Republican and represents the state of New York.

INGREDIENTS

3 tablespoons butter
½ cup corn oil
6 chicken cutlets
½ clove garlic, finely chopped
¼ teaspoon dried rosemary

¼ teaspoon dried oregano
¼ cup freshly squeezed lemon juice
Salt and pepper to taste
1 7-ounce can sliced mushrooms, drained
¼ cup chopped fresh parsley

1. Heat butter and oil in a heavy skillet over medium heat. When hot, add chicken cutlets and brown.

2. When cutlets are brown, add garlic, rosemary, oregano, and lemon juice, and salt and pepper to taste. Cover immediately. Simmer for 2–3 minutes.

3. Add mushrooms, cover again, and cook for 10–15 minutes.

4. Before serving, add chopped fresh parsley.

★★★★★★★★★★ **Fruited Chicken Salad** ★★★★★★★★★★

Submitted by Representative Steve Largent

SERVES 8

*C*ongressman Steve Largent is a Republican and represents the 1st District of Oklahoma.

INGREDIENTS

4 cups diced cooked chicken

2 cups seedless green grapes, or 1 15-
   ounce can pineapple chunks, drained

1 cup chopped celery

1 11-ounce can mandarin orange sections,
   drained

2 tablespoons grated onion, or onion
   powder to taste

1 cup mayonnaise

1 tablespoon prepared mustard

1 5-ounce can chow mein noodles

Lettuce leaves (for decoration)

1. In a large bowl, combine cooked chicken, grapes, celery, oranges, and onion.

2. Blend mayonnaise and mustard; toss gently with chicken mixture.

3. Cover and chill for several hours.

4. Just before serving, mix in chow mein noodles; turn salad into a lettuce-lined serving bowl.

45
★
Steve Largent

★★★★★★ **Marty Meehan's Chicken Picatta** ★★★★★★

Submitted by Representative Marty Meehan

SERVES 4–6

Congressman Marty Meehan is a Democrat and represents the 5th District of Massachusetts.

INGREDIENTS

8 thin boneless chicken fillets
2 eggs, beaten
Bread crumbs
Freshly grated Parmesan cheese
Butter
Oil

1½ cups chicken broth
¾ cup white wine
Juice of 6 lemons
1 pound fresh mushrooms, sliced
Ground pepper

1. Dip chicken into beaten eggs, then into a mixture of bread crumbs and freshly grated parmesan cheese.

2. Lightly brown chicken in a large skillet, using equal amounts of butter and oil. Drain liquid.

3. Add broth, wine, and fresh lemon juice. Cover skillet and simmer chicken for 1 hour, turning chicken occasionally.

4. In a small skillet, sauté mushrooms in butter until soft. Place on top of fillets.

5. Add ground pepper to taste.

********** **Honey-Mustard Chicken** **********

Submitted by Senator Frank Lautenberg

SERVES 4–6

*S*enator Frank Lautenberg is a Democrat and represents the state of New Jersey.

INGREDIENTS

1 stick margarine, melted
½ cup honey
¼ cup Dijon mustard

Salt and pepper to taste (optional)
1 3–4 pound chicken, cut up

1. Preheat oven to 350°.

2. Mix together margarine, honey, mustard, salt, and pepper. Pour over chicken pieces in a baking dish.

3. Bake uncovered for 60–75 minutes, or until nicely browned, basting often.

4. Serve with rice or couscous.

47
★

Frank Lautenberg

✶✶✶✶✶✶ **Dottie Miller's Oriental Chicken** ✶✶✶✶✶✶

Submitted by Representative Dave Weldon
From the Kitchen of Nancy Weldon

SERVES 6–8

66 *The meals we have shared with family and friends are a part of our wealth of memories. These recipes* are only a small sampling of the many gastronomical delights we have partaken of around the table. It is our hope that as the recipes are reproduced, the laughter, joy, and warmth of good food and faithful friends will also be reproduced. Nancy and I thank you for allowing us to share these treasures with others."*

—*Congressman Dave Weldon is a Republican and represents the 15th District of Florida.*

INGREDIENTS

6 large chicken breasts, boned
2 tablespoons flour
1 teaspoon garlic powder
2 tablespoons oil
½ cup chicken broth
1 20-ounce can pineapple chunks
½ teaspoon curry powder
½ teaspoon ground ginger

2 tablespoons cornstarch
¼ cup soy sauce
2 tablespoons ketchup
2 tablespoons vinegar
1 tablespoon honey
2 tablespoons sliced onion
6 ounces pea pods

1. Toss chicken breasts in flour and garlic powder; brown in heated oil. Add chicken broth and simmer for 15 minutes.

2. Drain pineapple and save juice. Combine ¼ of the pineapple juice with curry, ginger, and cornstarch. Blend in soy sauce, ketchup, vinegar, and honey. Pour over chicken. Simmer for 20 minutes.

3. Add remaining pineapple juice and more water if thick. Add pineapple chunks, onion, and pea pods, and cook for 5 minutes.

4. Serve over rice.

*Another recipe from the Weldon family appears on page 49.

★★★★★★★★ Amy Adam's Lemon Chicken ★★★★★★★★

Submitted by Representative Dave Weldon

SERVES 6–8

*C*ongressman Dave Weldon is a Republican and represents the 15th District of Florida.

INGREDIENTS

3 whole chicken breasts, skinned
3 chicken legs, skinned
3 chicken thighs, skinned
Salt and pepper
Paprika

Garlic powder
2 10 ¾-ounce cans chicken broth
3 tablespoons sherry
3 lemons (2 ounces), sliced

1. Preheat oven to 350°.

2. Arrange chicken in a baking dish. Sprinkle with salt and pepper, lots of paprika, and garlic powder.

3. Mix broth and sherry together. Put slices of lemon over chicken and pour soup mixture over all.

4. Bake for 1 hour.

49
★

Dave Weldon

★★★★★★★★★★★ **Korean Chicken** ★★★★★★★★★★★

Submitted by Senator Daniel K. Akaka

SERVES 6–8

Senator Daniel K. Akaka is a Democrat and represents the state of Hawaii.

INGREDIENTS

5 pounds chicken pieces
1 tablespoon salt
½–1 cup flour
Oil

SAUCE

1 stalk green onion, chopped
½ cup shoyu (Japanese soy sauce)
6 tablespoons sugar
1 clove garlic, chopped
1 teaspoon sesame oil
1 small red pepper, chopped (optional)

1. Salt chicken and refrigerate overnight.
2. Combine sauce ingredients in a saucepan over low heat and stir to dissolve sugar.
3. Roll chicken in flour and fry in oil.
4. After frying, dip in sauce and serve.

Lime and Cilantro Grilled
★★★★★★★ **Turkey Breast in Pita Pockets** ★★★★★★★

Submitted by Senator Richard Lugar

51
★
Richard Lugar

SERVES 10

66 *One of my family favorites. To enhance the meal, I usually serve a rice dish and spinach salad. This is an excellent meal to serve at a summer outing.*"
—*Senator Richard Lugar is a Republican and represents the state of Indiana.*

INGREDIENTS

1½ pounds turkey breast tenderloins
2 limes, juiced
1 tablespoon paprika
½ teaspoon onion salt
½ teaspoon garlic salt
½ teaspoon cayenne pepper
¼ teaspoon white pepper
½ teaspoon dried thyme
½ teaspoon fennel seeds
10 pitas, cut in half
1½ cups shredded lettuce
1½ cups Avocado Salsa
1½ cups Sour Cream Sauce (optional)

Avocado Salsa:

1 avocado, diced
1 lime, juiced
2 tomatoes, seeded and diced
½ cup minced green onion
½ cup minced green pepper
½ cup chopped fresh cilantro

Sour Cream Sauce:

1 cup sour cream
1 teaspoon salt
¼ cup minced green onion
¼ cup minced green chilies
¼ teaspoon cayenne pepper
½ teaspoon black pepper

1. Rub turkey with lime juice.

2. In a small bowl, combine paprika, onion salt, garlic salt, cayenne pepper, white pepper, thyme, and fennel seeds. Sprinkle mixture over turkey. Cover and refrigerate for at least 1 hour.

3. Preheat charcoal grill for direct-heat cooking.

4. Grill turkey 15–20 minutes, until meat thermometer reaches 170° and turkey is no longer pink in the center. Turn turkey over halfway through grilling time.

5. Allow turkey to stand 10 minutes. Slice into ¼-inch strips. Fill each pita half with turkey, lettuce, avocado salsa, and if desired, sour cream sauce.

Avocado Salsa:

1. In small bowl, combine avocado and lime juice. Stir in tomatoes, green onion, green pepper, and cilantro.
2. Cover and refrigerate until ready to use.

Sour Cream Sauce:

1. In small bowl, combine sour cream, salt, green onion, chilies, cayenne pepper, and black pepper.
2. Cover and refrigerate until ready to use.

★★★★★★★★★★★★ **Dove on the Grill** ★★★★★★★★★★★★

Submitted by Senator Richard Shelby

SERVES 2

66 *ne of my favorite activities is hunting. This is a simple yet delicious way to prepare wild dove.*"
—*Senator Richard Shelby is a Republican and represents the state of Alabama.*

53
★
Richard Shelby

Preparation Tip: If you are not a hunter, you may obtain wild dove from your butcher, or you may substitute Cornish game hen. The game hen is larger, so one hen per serving would be sufficient, wrapping each with a whole slice of bacon instead of half a slice.

INGREDIENTS
4 wild doves, cleaned and dressed
Salt, pepper, and Worcestershire sauce
    to taste
2 slices bacon

1. Sprinkle doves with salt, pepper, and Worcestershire sauce.
2. Wrap each dove with ½ slice bacon. Secure with toothpick if necessary.
3. Grill over medium fire until done, 20–30 minutes. Turn occasionally.

Variation:

1. Wrap ½ strip bacon around a water chestnut and a boneless dove breast.
2. Season lemon butter with Worcestershire sauce and baste frequently.
3. Grill or broil until bacon is done.

Pork and Lamb Dishes

★★★★★★★ Christmas Tortière (Pork Pie) ★★★★★★★

Submitted by Diane Milliken
From the Kitchen of Shelley Richard and Jeannette Camire

★

Diane Milliken

SERVES 4–6

66 *Pork Pie is a staple recipe for Americans of Canadian decent during the holiday season. My family in Maine would celebrate Christmas Eve into the wee hours of the night. The evening would begin with midnight Mass, with everyone coming to our home afterwards for the delightful meal we called The Reveillon. It always included Tortière, cranberry sauce, pickles, olives, stuffed celery, with an array of homemade nut breads and festive desserts. I truly hope that you will enjoy this recipe as much as I have over the years."*

Preparation Tip: Instead of using all ground pork, many choose to use half pork and half ground beef. Always use lean meat to cut down on the fat.

INGREDIENTS

1 pound lean ground pork
Water
1 medium onion, finely chopped
½ teaspoon salt
4–6 potatoes, peeled, cooked, and mashed (prepared without milk)

½ teaspoon cinnamon
1 teaspoon allspice
9-inch bottom and top pie crust

1. Break up pork in pan. Add enough water to almost cover pork. Add onion and salt. Cook over medium heat until all water is absorbed, stirring often, about 1½ hours.

2. While pork is cooking, preheat oven to 400°.

3. When pork is done, remove excess fat and add mashed potatoes, cinnamon, and allspice. Mix well.

4. Fill bottom pie crust with mixture and cover with top crust.

5. Bake for 30 minutes, or until well browned.

★★★★★★★★★★ **Sweet-Sour Spareribs** ★★★★★★★★★★

Submitted by Senator Daniel K. Akaka

SERVES 6–8

*S*enator Daniel K. Akaka is a Democrat and represents the state of Hawaii.

INGREDIENTS

5 pounds pork butt, cut into 1½-inch
    pieces
Flour
Oil
Pineapple chunks (optional)

Marinade:
½ cup shoyu (Japanese soy sauce)
1 tablespoon garlic salt
¼ teaspoon pepper
½ teaspoon ajinomoto (MSG) (optional)
Ground ginger (to taste)
Garlic powder (to taste)

Sauce:
2 cups sugar
1 cup vinegar
1½ cups water
¼ cup shoyu
2 teaspoons salt
1 teaspoon ajinomoto (optional)

1. Combine marinade ingredients and marinate pork overnight.

2. Dredge soaked pieces in flour and brown in oil.

3. Combine sauce ingredients and boil, then add pork. Simmer for 1 hour or until tender.

4. You may use pineapple chunks for a garnish. Add juice from pineapple chunks to sauce.

★★★★★★★ **Pork Chops and Spanish Rice** ★★★★★★★

Submitted by Representative Henry B. Gonzalez

SERVES 4

ongressman Henry B. Gonzalez is a Democrat and represents the 20th District of Texas.

INGREDIENTS

4 pork chops, 4 boneless, skinless chicken
  breast halves, or 1 pound lean ground
  beef
Garlic salt
Cayenne pepper
Black pepper
2 tablespoons cooking oil
1 cup uncooked white or brown rice
  (long-cooking)

1 medium onion, chopped
¼ cup chopped bell pepper
3 ounces tomato sauce
1 jalapeño or serrano pepper, chopped
  (optional)
Boiling water

1. Season pork chops to taste with garlic salt, cayenne, and black pepper.

2. In a heavy skillet, brown seasoned chops and set aside.

3. In a second skillet (or same skillet, cleaned) heat cooking oil over medium heat and add rice. Cook and stir rice until it loses its translucency and puffs (not until it turns brown, although a few pieces may be brown).

4. Stir in onion and pepper, then tomato sauce to which additional garlic salt, cayenne, and black pepper have been added.

5. Lay pork chops on top of rice mixture, add boiling water to cover, cover skillet, and cook until the water has been absorbed and the rice is done. Check periodically and add more boiling water if necessary.

Chicken Variation:

1. Chicken may be precooked by boiling gently for about 15 minutes or broiling slightly (about 10 minutes on each side), or you may use uncooked chicken.

2. Season chicken and lay on rice mixture.

3. Cook with the rice, adding boiling water as in Step 5 above, at a low-medium heat, until done. If chicken was boiled, use the cooking water for this step.

Ground Beef Variation:

1. Brown ground beef in skillet with seasonings, onion, and pepper.

2. Add meat mixture to rice just before rice is completely done, and all the water is absorbed.

60

**Pork and Lamb
Dishes**

★★★★★★★★★★★ **Pepper Pork Chops** ★★★★★★★★★★★

Submitted by Senator Alfonse D'Amato
From the Kitchen of Antoinette D'Amato

SERVES 4

*S*enator Alfonse D'Amato is a Republican and represents the state of New York.

INGREDIENTS

2 medium potatoes
4 tablespoons corn oil
6 medium pork chops
3 green bell peppers, sliced

3–4 vinegar peppers, sliced
¼ cup vinegar (from pepper jar)
Salt and pepper

1. Peel and cube potatoes, and boil until slightly tender.

2. In a heavy skillet, heat corn oil and brown pork chops.

3. Remove pork chops after browning, add sliced bell peppers, and cook until slightly tender.

4. Add pork chops and potatoes and cook for about 5 minutes.

5. Add sliced vinegar peppers and vinegar to skillet mixture, cover, and cook over medium heat for 5–10 minutes. Season with salt and pepper to taste.

Alfonse D'Amato

★★★★★★★★★★★★★★ **Pork Roast** ★★★★★★★★★★★★★★★

Submitted by Representative Doug Bereuter

SERVES 6–8

*C*ongressman *Doug Bereuter is a Republican and represents the 1st District of Nebraska.*

INGREDIENTS

1 boneless pork loin

2 cups cooked, cubed potatoes (optional)

2 cups cooked, cut-up carrots (optional)

1 12-ounce can Solo Apricot Filling, Solo Prune Filling, or sauerkraut

1. Preheat oven to 325°.

2. Place roast in pan (with a lid), surround with vegetables, and top with one of the fillings or sauerkraut. Topping will glaze pork and vegetables during baking.

3. Cover and bake for 30–45 minutes per pound (test for doneness with a meat thermometer).

★★★★★★★★★ Stuffed Iowa Pork Chops ★★★★★★★★★

Submitted by Senator Tom Harkin

★

Tom Harkin

SERVES 2

Senator Tom Harkin is a Democrat and represents the state of Iowa.

INGREDIENTS
½ cup whole kernel corn
½ cup bread crumbs
Pinch of salt and pepper
¾ tablespoon dried parsley
Pinch of sage
½ tablespoon chopped onion
½ cup diced peeled apple
1 tablespoon whole milk
2 Iowa pork chops (thick-cut)
Oil

Basting Sauce:
¼ cup honey
¼ cup mustard
¼ teaspoon rosemary leaves
½ teaspoon salt
Pinch of pepper

1. Preheat oven to 350°.
2. In a bowl, combine first 8 ingredients until well mixed.
3. Cut a slit in side of each chop and stuff with mixture.
4. In a separate bowl, combine basting ingredients and blend until smooth.
5. In a frying pan, brown stuffed chops in oil.
6. Transfer chops to a baking dish. Bake for about 1 hour, basting chops often with sauce.

★★★★★★★ **Braised or Broiled Pork Chops** ★★★★★★★

Submitted by Senator Lauch Faircloth
From the Kitchen of Bettye Cortner

SERVES 4

66 *One of my favorite dishes. . . . This dish brings back memories of good old North Carolina down-home cooking like I enjoyed as a young boy.*"
—Senator Lauch Faircloth is a Republican and represents the state of North Carolina.

INGREDIENTS

½ cup tomato juice
1 tablespoon Worcestershire sauce
½ teaspoon sugar
¼ teaspoon garlic salt
2 tablespoons cider vinegar

1 teaspoon prepared mustard
¼ teaspoon salt
¼ teaspoon hot sauce
4 1-inch-thick pork chops
1 tablespoon vegetable oil

1. Combine first 8 ingredients and set aside.

To Braise Chops:

1. Brown on both sides in oil in a large nonstick skillet. Remove from skillet and drain.
2. Return pork chops to skillet; add tomato juice mixture.
3. Bring mixture to a boil; cover, reduce heat, and simmer 15 minutes.

To Broil Chops:

1. Place pork chops on lightly greased rack of broiler pan; brush with tomato juice mixture.
2. Broil 4–5 inches from heat for 15 minutes, turning once and brushing occasionally with sauce.

✶✶✶✶✶✶✶✶✶ **Roast Leg of Spring Lamb** ✶✶✶✶✶✶✶✶✶

Submitted by Senator Rick Santorum

SERVES 8

$\mathcal{S}$enator Rick Santorum is a Republican and represents the state of Pennsylvania.

INGREDIENTS

1 5-pound leg of lamb

10–15 cloves garlic, peeled and slivered

1 teaspoon cracked black pepper

2 teaspoons dried rosemary

1 10½-ounce can beef bouillon
  (double strength is fine)

1 pint dry red wine

1 pint whipping cream

65

✶

Rick Santorum

1. Preheat oven to 450°.

2. Remove excess fat from the lamb. Remove hip bone and knee socket, leaving only the femur in the center of the leg. (The butcher will often do this for you.) With a sharp paring knife, make about 30 sharp stabs and insert a generous sliver of garlic in each opening. (This can be done several hours before baking time.)

3. Place lamb in an open baking pan on a wire rack with fat side up. Sprinkle half the cracked pepper on the upper surface. Bake uncovered for 20–25 minutes.

4. Turn meat and sprinkle top with remaining cracked pepper. Bake uncovered for another 20–25 minutes.

5. Turn oven down to 400°.

6. Drain excess fat from pan. Turn leg to the original top side and sprinkle with rosemary.

7. Bring bouillon and wine to a boil, add to roasting pan, and cover.

8. Bake for another 20–30 minutes. (Total cooking time should be 70–90 minutes.)

9. Remove lamb and wire rack. Bring sauce to a boil on the top of the stove and reduce. Strain and reduce sauce further, until sauce is syrupy and will lightly coat a spoon. Add cream and reduce (by cooking briskly) to desired consistency.

10. Slice lamb thinly and serve over a pool of sauce on heated plates.

Fish and Seafood Dishes

★★★★★★★★★★★★★★★ Fish Dijon ★★★★★★★★★★★★★★★

Submitted by Senator Connie Mack

SERVES 4

This recipe is one of Senator Mack's favorites and was taken from The Good Book of Nutrition.*

—*Senator Connie Mack is a Republican and represents the state of Florida.*

Connie Mack

INGREDIENTS

1 pound boneless fish fillets
2 tablespoons Dijon mustard
½ cup cooked brown rice
⅓ cup chopped fresh parsley
⅓ cup chopped red onion
⅓ cup chopped green bell pepper

⅓ cup fish or chicken broth, either homemade or canned
½ cup shredded part-skim mozzarella cheese
⅓ cup bread crumbs
Paprika to taste

1. Preheat oven to 350°.

2. Spray an 8 x 8 baking dish with nonstick cooking spray. In prepared dish, arrange half the fillets in a single layer. Spread with mustard. Layer rice, parsley, onion, and green pepper over fillets. Arrange remaining fillets over layers. Pour broth over top.

3. Sprinkle with cheese, bread crumbs, and paprika. Bake for 15 minutes.

4. Serve immediately.

*Nashville, Tenn.: Great American Opportunities, 1987. Recipe contains approximately per serving: 213 calories; 4.1 grams of fat; 17.32 percent calories from fat. Used with the permission of the American Cancer Society.

★★★★★ **Sautéed Trout with Fresh Tarragon** ★★★★★

Submitted by Senator Daniel Patrick Moynihan

SERVES 2

*S*enator Daniel Patrick Moynihan is a Democrat and represents the state of
New York.

INGREDIENTS

4 tablespoons butter
2 small brook trout, gutted, washed, and
  dried with paper towels
Fresh tarragon leaves (generous handful),
  roughly cut

Salt and pepper to taste
Juice of 1 lemon

1. In a frying pan large enough to hold both fish, melt butter until nut-brown in
color, carefully watching so as not to burn butter. Add fish, tarragon, salt and pepper,
and lemon juice, and cook on one side for about 3½ minutes.

2. Turn trout gently with 2 wooden spatulas and continue to cook for 4–5 minutes,
or until springy when touched and flesh is flaky.

3. Remove fish from pan and fillet it: Insert a sharp knife at the back of the head.
Run knife along the back and underside, cutting on to the bone, and the whole bone
will be exposed. Lift tail and it will come off intact with the head.

4. Place fillets on plates and top with sauce from pan.

★★★★★★★★★★★ Catfish Casserole ★★★★★★★★★★★★

Submitted by Senator Trent Lott

SERVES 6

*S*enator Trent Lott is a Republican and represents the state of Mississippi.

INGREDIENTS

1 10-ounce package frozen chopped spinach, thawed
Salt and pepper to taste
6 small catfish fillets (or substitute flounder or sole)
¼ pound fresh mushrooms, sliced
1 small onion, chopped
1 tablespoon butter

White Sauce:

3 tablespoons butter
2 tablespoons flour
1 cup milk
¼ cup white wine (optional)
¼ cup grated Parmesan cheese

1. Preheat oven to 375°.

2. Put chopped spinach in the bottom of a buttered casserole dish, blotting it slightly to absorb extra water. Add salt and pepper to taste.

3. Arrange catfish on top of spinach in a single layer.

4. Sauté mushrooms and onion in butter and pour over fish.

5. Prepare white sauce: Melt butter in a saucepan and stir in flour. Slowly add milk, then wine. Heat until thick, then add Parmesan cheese.

6. Pour white sauce over casserole. Bake for 20–25 minutes, or until it bubbles.

★★★★★★★★★★★★★★ **Red Snapper** ★★★★★★★★★★★★★★★

Submitted by Senator Sam Nunn

SERVES 4

$\mathcal{S}$*enator Sam Nunn is a Democrat and represents the state of Georgia.*

Preparation Tip: You may substitute any white fish if red snapper is not available in your area; North Atlantic perch works well.

INGREDIENTS

½ cup minced onion
3 tablespoons fresh orange juice
2 tablespoons oil
2 teaspoons grated orange peel

1 teaspoon salt
4 red snapper fillets
Dash of nutmeg and ground pepper

1. Combine onion, orange juice, oil, orange peel, and salt in greased 12 x 8 x 2 pan. Arrange snapper fillets in this mixture, turning to coat evenly.

2. Marinate at room temperature for 30 minutes, lightly covered.

3. Preheat oven to 400°.

4. Sprinkle fish with nutmeg and pepper. Bake for about 12 minutes, or until fillets flake easily.

5. Baste. Serve immediately.

★★★★★★ **San Francisco Seasoned Shrimp** ★★★★★★

Submitted by Senator Dianne Feinstein

SERVES 4

❝*T*angy and tasty. Enjoy!"*
—Senator Dianne Feinstein is a Democrat and represents the state of California.*

73
★

Dianne Feinstein

INGREDIENTS

2 tablespoons lemon juice

Salt and pepper to taste

3 tablespoons olive oil

1 pound shrimp

1 large onion

3 tablespoons pimiento (from a jar)

¼ cup sliced olives

1 lemon, cut into wedges

1. Mix lemon juice, salt, black pepper, and olive oil. Set aside.

2. Cook shrimp and shell it.

3. Set shrimp in marinade and let sit for at least 2–3 hours. If you can wait, do it overnight (in the refrigerator).

4. Slice onion into rings and mix with marinated shrimp. Add pimiento and olive slices just before serving. Serve lemon wedges on the side.

★★★★★★★★★★★★ **Seville Shrimp** ★★★★★★★★★★★★★

Submitted by Senator Bob Dole

★

Fish and Seafood

Dishes

SERVES 4

Former Senator Bob Dole is a Republican and represented the state of Kansas.

INGREDIENTS

¾ cup margarine

½ cup grated Parmesan cheese

½ cup dry bread crumbs

¼ cup lemon juice

⅔ cup chopped green onions

1 clove garlic, minced

¼ teaspoon salt

1 pound cooked small shrimp

Fresh parsley, chopped

1. Preheat oven to 350°.
2. Combine all ingredients. Place in 4 individual casserole dishes.
3. Bake for 20–23 minutes.
4. Garnish with fresh parsley and additional shrimp if desired.

Garithes Me Lemoni Ke Lathee
★★★★★ **(Shrimp with Lemon and Olive Oil)** ★★★★★

Submitted by Representative Michael Bilirakis

SERVES 4

*C*ongressman Michael Bilirakis is a Republican and represents the 9th District of Florida.

INGREDIENTS

4 cloves garlic, chopped
½ cup olive oil
1 pound large shrimp, unpeeled
½ cup lemon juice

½ cup wine
1 teaspoon salt
1 tablespoon pepper

1. In a large frying pan, sauté garlic in olive oil. Add shrimp and cook until shrimp are pink, stirring continuously.

2. When shrimp are cooked, add lemon juice, wine, salt, and pepper, and stir.

3. Serve with fresh Greek bread and salad.

75
★

Michael Bilirakis

★★★★★★★★★ **Frank's Favorite Scallops** ★★★★★★★★★

Submitted by Senator Frank H. Murkowski

SERVES 6

❝*My favorite recipe is Frank's Favorite Scallops, of course! This recipe represents the tradition of good seafood in Alaska and is one my son-in-law often prepares for me.*❞
—*Senator Frank H. Murkowski is a Republican and represents the state of Alaska.*

INGREDIENTS

½ cup butter
1 shallot, chopped
2 pounds fresh chanterelle mushrooms, chopped
¼ cup white port wine
¼ cup chopped chives

½ cup butter
2½ pounds scallops
Freshly ground pepper
¼ cup white port wine
¼ cup chopped chives

1. Melt first ½ cup butter in a saucepan. Add shallot and mushrooms, and cook until soft, about 10 minutes, on medium-low heat.

2. Remove from heat, add ¼ cup wine and ¼ cup chives. Heat until hot.

3. Melt second ½ cup butter in a heavy skillet. Add scallops, season with pepper, and sauté until scallops turn white and begin to lose translucency, about 10 minutes.

4. Remove from heat, add remaining port wine and chives.

5. Add prepared sauce and heat through.

★★★★★ John Warner's Norfolk Crab Cakes ★★★★★

Submitted by Senator John Warner

" *Chef's Note: This is a recipe in which the precise measurements, preparation of the mix, and cooking variables are trade secrets known only to the chef! Traditional crab cakes are those made with a mix of the ingredients recommended below and amounts to suit the chef's particular taste.* "
—*Senator John Warner is a Republican and represents the state of Virginia.*

John Warner

Preparation Tip: This recipe was tested by Bonnie Brace with great success. She just used the pinch-and-taste method of cooking once used by our mothers: they tasted the food as they went along in the recipe until they achieved the taste and texture they were looking for. Be adventurous with this recipe, and keep trying different amounts until the crab cakes are the way you personally want them to taste. Have fun!

INGREDIENTS

Fresh onions, preferably at least 2 types for a variety of flavor and texture, chopped	*Bread crumbs*
	Ground black pepper
	Vegetable salt
1 tablespoon butter	*Heavy cream*
Green bell peppers, chopped	*Fresh butter*
Fresh Chesapeake Bay blue-crab meat	*Fresh parsley, chopped*
Eggs, beaten	

1. Sauté onions in 1 tablespoon butter, taking care not to lose firmness or texture. Slightly sauté green bell peppers to release full flavor.

2. Mix crab, eggs, cooked onions and peppers, bread crumbs, black pepper, and small amount of salt (often crab meat is naturally salty).

3. Add sufficient cream to bind mixture lightly.

4. Form into cakes.

5. Cook butter until brown and quickly add parsley to release parsley's natural flavor.

6. Drop cakes into butter, cooking sparingly so as not to lose the fresh crab flavor. Turn once.

7. Remove and serve.

★★★★★★★★★★ **Baked Shad and Roe** ★★★★★★★★★★

Submitted by Senator William V. Roth, Jr.

SERVES 2

$\mathcal{S}$enator William V. Roth, Jr., is a Republican and represents the state of Delaware.

Note: This dish is a delicacy and is served in many fine restaurants around the country. The fish eggs, or roe, are available only in the spring, and only in certain regions, which makes the dish a rarity. Because the roe's availability did not coincide with the deadline for this cookbook, this recipe was not tested.

INGREDIENTS

1 medium-to-large shad, cleaned, split,
* and boned*
1 set shad roe

½ pint sour cream
Paprika
Lemon slices

1. Preheat oven to 400°.
2. Place fish in a shallow, greased baking dish, skin side down.
3. Top fish with roe, cover fish and roe with a thick layer of sour cream, and sprinkle with paprika.
4. Put 2 thin lemon slices on each piece of fish.
5. Bake 30 minutes.

★★★★★★★ **Sautéed Shrimp and Scallops** ★★★★★★★

Submitted by Senator Rick Santorum

SERVES 4

*S*enator Rick Santorum is a Republican and represents the state of Pennsylvania.

Preparation Tip: This can also be made into a delicious thick soup.

79

★

Rick Santorum

INGREDIENTS

½ pound fresh bay scallops
½ pound fresh or frozen shrimp
6 small green onions, chopped
¼ cup chopped shallots
3 tablespoons butter
3 cloves garlic, minced
2 ½ teaspoons dried basil leaves

½ teaspoon dried tarragon
½ teaspoon dried chervil
¼ teaspoon dried thyme
½ cup dry white wine
¼ cup chopped fresh parsley
Freshly ground black pepper

1. Clean fibrous portion from scallops, wash briefly in cold water, and drain.

2. Clean or thaw shrimp and cut into scallop-size segments.

3. Sauté scallions and shallots in butter and add garlic and dried herbs. (If fresh herb leaves are used, quantity should be quadrupled and added later with parsley.)

4. Add wine and stir. Bring sauce to a boil and reduce by half.

5. Add shrimp, scallops, fresh parsley, and black pepper. Sauté for no more than 10 minutes (less if scallops are small). Liquid volume will be greatly increased by juice of shellfish.

6. Lift shrimp and scallops from sauce and set aside while sauce is further reduced.

To Make Soup:

1. Do not reduce sauce in steps 4 and 6 above.

2. Serve with toasted French bread.

Vegetable Dishes

★★★★★★★★★★★★★★ **Texas Potatoes** ★★★★★★★★★★★★★★

Submitted by Representative Barbara Cubin

SERVES 8–10

*C*ongresswoman Barbara Cubin is a Republican and represents, at large, the state of Wyoming.

INGREDIENTS

3 20-ounce packages frozen hash brown
    potatoes, separated
¾–1 cup chopped onions
1 pint sour cream
¾ cup melted butter

1 10¾-ounce can cream of chicken soup
Dash of salt and pepper
2 cups crushed corn flakes

83
★
Barbara Cubin

1. Preheat oven to 350°.
2. Mix together all ingredients except corn flakes and ¼ cup melted butter and spread in a large baking pan.
3. Top with corn flakes and remaining melted butter.
4. Bake uncovered for 45 minutes.

★★★★★★★★★★ **Hash Brown Casserole** ★★★★★★★★★★★

Submitted by Representative Tom Latham
From the Kitchen of Kathy Latham

SERVES 8–10

Congressman Tom Latham is a Republican and represents the 5th District of Iowa.

Preparation Tip: This dish may be made in advance and either refrigerated or frozen. Hash browns need not be thawed before preparing. You can cut down the fat considerably in this recipe by using fat-free or reduced-fat sour cream, cheddar cheese, and whipping cream.

INGREDIENTS

½ cup butter or margarine
½ cup chopped onion
1 tablespoon salt
½ pint whipping cream
1 10¾-ounce can cream of chicken soup

8 ounces sour cream
2 cups shredded cheddar cheese
2 pounds frozen hash brown potatoes
2 cups Rice Krispies

1. Preheat oven to 350°.
2. Melt ¼ cup butter and sauté chopped onion.
3. Remove from heat and mix in salt, whipping cream, chicken soup, sour cream, and cheddar cheese.
4. Spread hash browns in 9 x 13 baking pan and cover with above mixture.
5. Melt remaining ¼ cup butter and coat Rice Krispies, then spread over mixture.
6. Bake uncovered for 1 hour.

★★★★★★★★★★ **Potatoes à la Bernice** ★★★★★★★★★★

Submitted by Senator Dirk Kempthorne

SERVES 8–10

*S*enator *Dirk Kempthorne is a Republican and represents the state of Idaho.*

★

Dirk Kempthorne

INGREDIENTS

2 pounds frozen hash brown potatoes
1 cup chopped onions
1 10¾-ounce can cream of mushroom
*   soup*
2 cups sour cream
2 cups grated sharp cheese

1 teaspoon salt
¼ teaspoon pepper
2 cups crushed potato chips
½ cup melted butter

1. Mix all ingredients except potato chips and butter together in a 9 x 13 baking dish. Refrigerate. (This can be done the night before.)

2. Before baking, preheat oven to 350°.

3. Combine crushed potato chips and melted butter and pour over top of casserole.

4. Bake uncovered for 1 hour.

★★★★★★★★★★★★★★ **Tamale Corn** ★★★★★★★★★★★★★★★

Submitted by Representative Barbara Cubin

SERVES 4–6

*C*ongresswoman Barbara Cubin is a Republican and represents, at large, the state of Wyoming.

INGREDIENTS

1 medium onion, chopped
2 green onions, chopped
¼ cup chopped green pepper
1 stalk celery, chopped
3 tablespoons butter

1 16½-ounce can of corn
6 canned tamales
Chili powder to taste
Salt and pepper to taste

1. Preheat oven to 350°.
2. Sauté onions, green pepper, and celery in butter until tender.
3. Drain corn and add to sautéed vegetables. Heat until warmed through.
4. Slice tamales in half lengthwise.
5. Layer tamales and corn mixture, sprinkling each layer with chili powder and salt and pepper. Begin with tamales and end with corn on top. Sprinkle top with chili powder.
6. Bake approximately 30 minutes, until browned and hot throughout.

★★★★★★★★ **Spanakopita (Spinach Pie)** ★★★★★★★★

Submitted by Representative Michael Bilirakis

★
Michael Bilirakis

SERVES 6–8

*C*ongressman Michael Bilirakis is a Republican and represents the 9th District of Florida.

INGREDIENTS

1 10-ounce package frozen chopped spinach
2 eggs, beaten
⅓ cup feta cheese
1 tablespoon cream cheese
1 tablespoon grated Romano cheese

½ cup cottage cheese
1 small onion, grated
Salt and pepper to taste
⅓ pound phyllo dough
½ stick butter or margarine, melted

1. Preheat oven to 375°–400°.

2. Thaw and drain spinach, squeezing out all liquid.

3. Place eggs and cheeses in a mixing bowl and bring to room temperature. Add spinach, onion, and salt and pepper and mix thoroughly.

4. Grease an 8-inch pie pan with margarine.

5. Place rectangular sheets of phyllo on pan one at a time at 45° angles in a criss-cross pattern, buttering each sheet, spreading it with spinach mixture, folding over, and sealing along edges as you go along. Save one last sheet for the top.

6. Place the last sheet on top and fold all the sheets in to fit the pan, as in making a pie.

7. Tuck any remaining edges of phyllo in along sides of pan with dull side of knife. Cut 4 lines about ¼-inch deep across top of phyllo. Paint top with remaining butter.

8. Bake for 30 minutes.

9. Cut into serving pieces and serve hot or cold.

★★★★★★★★★★★★ **Stuffed Cabbage** ★★★★★★★★★★★★

Submitted by Senator Carl Levin

SERVES 6

$\mathcal{S}$*enator Carl Levin is a Democrat and represents the state of Michigan.*

Preparation Tip: To remove cabbage leaves from head, cut stem close enough that leaves begin to loosen; dip head in boiling water and pull off leaves as they begin to loosen.

INGREDIENTS

6 large cabbage leaves
1 pound ground beef
¼ cup uncooked rice
1 egg, beaten
Grated onion or onion powder to taste

¼ teaspoon salt
¼ cup lemon juice and/or vinegar
¼–½ cup brown sugar
1 cup tomato sauce
Water or tomato juice to cover

1. Blanch cabbage leaves by boiling 2 minutes; rinse in cold water.

2. Combine ground beef, rice, egg, grated onion, and salt.

3. Roll mixture in steamed cabbage leaves.

4. Place rolls in large skillet with lemon juice, brown sugar, tomato sauce, and water to cover.

5. Simmer at least 1 hour, but longer if possible (as long as several hours).

Can be frozen.

★★★★★★★★★ **French-Cut String Beans** ★★★★★★★★★

Submitted by Senator Alfonse D'Amato
From the Kitchen of Antoinette D'Amato

SERVES 4

$\mathcal{S}$enator Alfonse D'Amato is a Republican and represents the state of New York.

89
★
Alfonse D'Amato

INGREDIENTS

1 pound fresh string beans
¼ cup water
¼ cup corn oil
5 tablespoons tomato sauce
1 teaspoon dried oregano

1 clove garlic, finely chopped
¼ cup grated Romano or Parmesan
* cheese*
Salt and pepper to taste

1. Wash string beans and drain. Slice beans French style (lengthwise).

2. Place sliced beans in heavy skillet, adding water, oil, tomato sauce, oregano, garlic, and grated cheese. Season with salt and pepper to taste.

3. Cover skillet tightly. Cook over low-medium heat for about 20 minutes, or until beans are slightly firm but tender.

★★★★★★★★ **Beets in Sour Cream Sauce** ★★★★★★★★

Submitted by Representative Philip M. Crane

SERVES 4

Congressman Philip M. Crane is a Republican and represents the 8th District of Illinois.

INGREDIENTS

2½ cups sliced beets, cooked and drained

Sauce:

¼ cup sour cream

1 tablespoon vinegar

1 teaspoon chopped green onions (tops and bottoms)

¾ teaspoon sugar

½ teaspoon salt

Dash of cayenne

1. Combine sauce ingredients in a large saucepan. Add cooked beets, and stir to coat each beet evenly.

2. Heat slowly, stirring now and then, but do not boil.

Beans and Rice

 **Hoppin' John**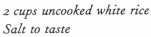

Submitted by Senator Mitch McConnell

SERVES 8

*S*enator Mitch McConnell is a Republican and represents the state of Kentucky.

INGREDIENTS

2 cups dried or frozen black-eyed peas
¼ pound bacon
2 small hot red peppers

2 cups uncooked white rice
Salt to taste

93
★

Mitch McConnell

1. Cover peas with water. Simmer peas, bacon, and peppers in a covered pot over low heat for 1–1½ hours, or until tender.

2. Add rice, cover, and cook over low heat, stirring frequently, until rice is cooked. Add more water during cooking if necessary.

3. Add salt to desired taste.

★★★★★★★★★★ **Arizona Baked Beans** ★★★★★★★★★★

Submitted by Senator John McCain

SERVES 6–8

Senator John McCain is a Republican and represents the state of Arizona.

INGREDIENTS

1 medium onion, chopped
1 teaspoon butter
1 16-ounce can red kidney beans
1 16-ounce can B&M baked beans
1 cup ketchup

1 cup packed brown sugar
1 teaspoon vinegar
1 teaspoon French's yellow mustard
4 strips fried bacon, cooled and crumbled

1. Preheat oven to 350°–375°.
2. In a skillet, sauté chopped onion in butter.
3. In a large baking pot, combine kidney beans, baked beans, ketchup, brown sugar, vinegar, mustard, and crumbled bacon. Add sautéed onions and mix well.
4. Bake in a covered dish for 35 minutes, or until piping hot.

★★★★★ Phil Gramm's Award-Winning Chili ★★★★★

Submitted by Senator Phil Gramm

★
Phil Gramm

SERVES 6–8

*S*enator *Phil Gramm is a Republican and represents the state of Texas.*

INGREDIENTS

1 pound lean ground beef

*1 pound beef tenderloins, cut up into
   sugar-cube-sized chunks*

*1 small onion, minced, or 1 heaping
   tablespoon dehydrated onion*

2 8-ounce cans tomato sauce

2 cups water

4 tablespoons chili powder

1–2 teaspoons salt

2 teaspoons paprika (optional)

1 tablespoon ground cumin (optional)

½–1 teaspoon cayenne pepper (optional)

2 cloves garlic, minced

2–3 tablespoons flour

1. In a skillet, brown ground beef, beef tenderloin, and onion. Drain if necessary.

2. Add tomato sauce, water, chili powder, salt, paprika, cumin, red pepper, and garlic.
Cook for 1–2 hours.

3. Stir in flour. Cook another 15 minutes.

★★★★★★★★★★★★★ Cincinnati Chili ★★★★★★★★★★★★★

Submitted by Representative Michael G. Oxley

SERVES 6

*C*ongressman *Michael G. Oxley is a Republican and represents the 4th District of Ohio.*

INGREDIENTS

2 tablespoons butter

2 pounds lean ground beef

6 bay leaves

1 large onion, chopped

6 cloves garlic, minced

1 teaspoon cinnamon

2 teaspoons allspice

4 teaspoons vinegar

1 teaspoon dried red pepper flakes, crushed, or chili caribe

1 teaspoon salt

2 tablespoons pure red chili powder

1 teaspoon ground cumin

1 teaspoon dried oregano

1 6-ounce can tomato paste

6 cups water

8 ounces vermicelli, cooked

1 15-ounce can kidney beans, drained and rinsed

½ cup grated cheddar cheese

1 small onion, finely chopped

1. Heat butter in skillet over medium-high heat. Add meat, stirring until evenly browned.

2. Transfer to larger pot and stir in all remaining ingredients up through water. Taste and adjust seasonings. If too sweet, add vinegar.

3. Bring to a boil, lower heat, and simmer uncovered for 2–4 hours.

4. Add kidney beans ¼ hour before serving.

5. Serve in individual bowls over cooked vermicelli. Top with grated cheese and raw onion.

✯✯✯✯✯✯✯✯✯✯ **Baked Lima Beans** ✯✯✯✯✯✯✯✯✯✯

Submitted by Senator Jesse Helms

97

✯

Jesse Helms

SERVES 4

*S*enator Jesse Helms is a Republican and represents the state of North Carolina.

INGREDIENTS

2 cups dried lima beans

2 quarts water

1 medium onion, chopped

1 cup chopped canned whole tomatoes
   with juice

1 teaspoon mustard

1 green pepper, chopped

2 teaspoons salt

2 tablespoons brown sugar

4 slices bacon

1. Soak beans overnight in cold water. Drain. Add water and boil until tender, about 1½ hours.

2. While beans are cooking, preheat oven to 325°.

3. Pour beans into buttered casserole. Add next 6 ingredients. Put bacon on top.

4. Bake covered for 2 hours.

5. Uncover for last 20 minutes. Add water if necessary.

★★★★★★★★ **Searchlight Beans and Rice** ★★★★★★★★

Submitted by Senator Harry Reid

SERVES 6–8

66 *A* *one-pot, easy meal passed along to me from my dad, who would cook pots of beans to sustain his long days underground in the mines of southern Nevada. Although we made the cost-effective beans a year-round meal for my family, it's now a popular low-fat, high-fiber alternative for the eves of Thanksgiving and/or Christmas. Helps keep the refrigerator clear for all the holiday fixins!"*

—*Senator Harry Reid is a Democrat and represents the state of Nevada.*

Preparation Tip: Use spices in quantities that approximate the taste you desire. Serve piping hot alongside a heap of white rice. A dash of salt may enhance flavor. Garnish with salsa, tortillas, or other optional sides. Great for cold desert nights!

INGREDIENTS

1 pound dried pinto beans (soak as
   directed on package; do not drain)
2 cups cubed precooked ham
1 small onion, chopped
1 bell pepper, chopped
1 tablespoon chili powder

½ teaspoon black pepper
1 teaspoon ground cumin
½ teaspoon dried rosemary
½ teaspoon dried thyme
½ teaspoon dried tarragon
Cooked white rice

1. Combine all ingredients except rice.
2. Cook over low heat for 6–8 hours.
3. Serve with white rice.

★★★★★★★★ **Wild Rice and Mushrooms** ★★★★★★★★

Submitted by Representative George R. Nethercutt, Jr.

SERVES 8–10

C̸ongressman George R. Nethercutt, Jr., is a Republican and represents the state of Washington.

INGREDIENTS

½ pound wild rice
Dash salt
¾ pound fresh mushrooms, sliced
½ pound butter or margarine
2 teaspoons flour

½ pint whipping cream
Salt and pepper to taste
½ cup dry sherry or sherry flavoring
Buttered bread crumbs

**George R.
Nethercutt, Jr.**

1. Preheat oven to 350°.

2. Wash and drain rice, and cook according to package directions until tender, about 30 minutes. Drain.

3. Meanwhile, sauté mushrooms in butter. Add flour and cream, stirring constantly. Season with salt and pepper.

4. Add cooked rice, and stir in sherry. Do not overcook.

5. Put in well-greased casserole, and top with buttered crumbs.

6. Bake until heated through and light brown on top.

7. If dish is to be reheated, add more cream.

★★★★★★ **Grandma Daigle's Rice Dressing** ★★★★★★

Submitted by Senator John Breaux

SERVES 10–12

*S*enator John Breaux is a Republican and represents the state of Louisiana.

INGREDIENTS

1 pound lean ground beef
3 tablespoons cooking oil
1 cup chopped onion
½ cup chopped green onion tops
1 cup chopped celery
1 large bell pepper, chopped

½ cup chopped fresh parsley
1 cup water
3 cups cooked rice
Salt and pepper to taste
2 tablespoons Kitchen Bouquet (optional)

1. Cook meat in oil in a large pot until brown.

2. Add onions, celery, bell pepper, and parsley. Reduce heat and cook until vegetables are wilted. Add water and stir to combine. If needed, add more water to keep about the same amount of liquid that you started with.

3. Stir in cooked rice and keep warm until ready to serve.

★★★★★★★★★★ Pistachio Rice Pilaf ★★★★★★★★★★

Submitted by Senator Joseph Lieberman

SERVES 6

"*My wife's and my favorite recipe.*"
—*Senator Joseph Lieberman is a Democrat and represents the state of Connecticut.*

INGREDIENTS

¼ cup currants
1 cup long-grain brown rice
2 cups water or vegetable broth

½ cup unsalted pistachio nuts
¼ cup dried apricots, cut into strips
Dash of cinnamon

1. Soak currants for 15 minutes in warm water. Drain and set aside.

2. Wash rice and drain. Place in a skillet over medium heat and stir around until it is dry and lightly browned (be careful not to burn!).

3. Place toasted rice in a 1½-quart saucepan and cover with water or broth. Bring to a boil, reduce heat to low, and cover with a tight-fitting lid.

4. After rice has simmered for about 25 minutes, place the currants, apricots, and nuts on top of the rice (do not stir in). Return the lid and continue simmering another 20 minutes, or until rice is tender and water is absorbed.

5. Remove from heat and let stand 2 minutes. Turn into a serving dish. Sprinkle cinnamon over the top.

★

Joseph Lieberman

★★★★★★★★★★★★★★ **Baked Rice** ★★★★★★★★★★★★★★

Submitted by Senator Alfonse D'Amato
From the Kitchen of Antoinette D'Amato

SERVES 4

Senator Alfonse D'Amato is a Republican and represents the state of New York.

Preparation Tip: Fresh sliced mushrooms may be added before baking.

INGREDIENTS

6 tablespoons butter
1 cup long-grain white rice
4 chicken bouillon cubes
5 cups boiling water
¼ cup grated cheddar, Romano, or any
  hard cheese

1 green bell pepper, chopped
1 clove garlic, finely chopped
Ground pepper to taste

1. Preheat oven to 350°.

2. Melt butter in heavy skillet and evenly brown rice.

3. In casserole dish, dissolve bouillon cubes in boiling water. Stir until completely dissolved.

4. Stir browned rice into casserole mixture. Add cheese, bell pepper, garlic, and ground pepper.

5. Cover and bake for 30 minutes.

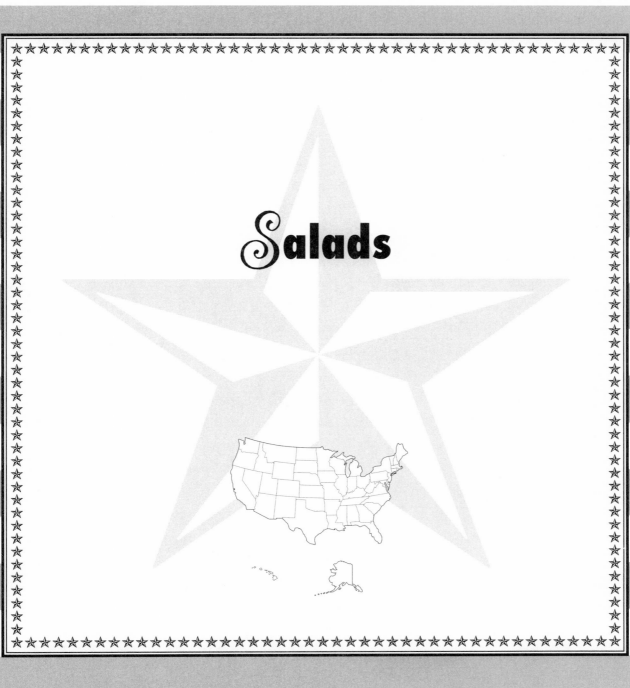

Salads

✶✶✶✶✶✶✶✶✶ **Strawberry-Spinach Salad** ✶✶✶✶✶✶✶✶✶✶

Submitted by Representative John A. Boehner

SERVES 6–8

❝The 8th District of Ohio has several large fruit farms that raise delicious strawberries. The following recipe is one we have enjoyed. . . .❞
—Congressman John A. Boehner is a Republican and represents the 8th District of Ohio.

✶

John A. Boehner

INGREDIENTS

½ pound fresh spinach, washed, patted dry, and torn into small pieces
½ pound Bibb lettuce, washed, patted dry, and torn into small pieces
1 pint fresh strawberries, hulled and halved
¾ cup pecan halves, browned in butter

Dressing:

⅓ cup raspberry vinegar
¼ teaspoon salt
¼ cup sugar
1 tablespoon poppy seeds
1 teaspoon dry mustard
2 teaspoons minced onion
1 cup light vegetable oil

1. Combine spinach and lettuce in large bowl.

2. Mix dressing ingredients together very well. Pour over spinach and lettuce mixture; toss.

3. Arrange lettuce mixture into individual salad bowls and top with pecans and strawberries.

★★★★★★★★★★★★ **Vegetable Salad** ★★★★★★★★★★★★

Submitted by Senator Sam Nunn
From the Kitchen of Colleen Nunn

SERVES 6

*S*enator Sam Nunn is a Democrat and represents the state of Georgia.

INGREDIENTS

1 11-ounce can white corn
1 14½-ounce can cut green beans
1 15-ounce can English peas
1 14-ounce can La Choy Fancy Chinese
 Vegetables
1½ cups chopped celery
1 medium sweet onion, chopped
1 2-ounce package slivered almonds
 (toasted)

Marinade:

⅓ cup sugar
¼ cup dark vinegar
½ cup salad oil
1 teaspoon salt
1 teaspoon black pepper

1. Drain canned vegetables and mix with celery, onion, and almonds.
2. Mix marinade ingredients together and pour over vegetables.
3. Marinate in refrigerator for several hours before serving.

★★★★★★★★★★★★ **Broccoli Salad** ★★★★★★★★★★★★

Submitted by Senator Bob Smith
From the Kitchen of Mary Jo Smith

SERVES 6

66 *This dish is always a hit at potluck gatherings.*"
—*Senator Bob Smith is a Republican and represents the state of New Hampshire.*

INGREDIENTS

1 bunch broccoli

½ cup chopped onion (optional)

8 strips bacon, fried, drained, and crumbled, or ½ cup chopped nuts or seeds (walnuts, sunflower seeds, etc.)

¾ cup mayonnaise

¼ cup sugar

2 tablespoons vinegar

½ cup raisins

1. Cut broccoli into bite-size pieces, peeling stalk prior to cutting up.

2. Mix with onions and bacon or nuts and set aside.

3. Combine mayonnaise, sugar, and vinegar. Pour over broccoli mixture, and toss gently.

4. Stir in raisins and toss again. Chill.

Breads

The Grassley Family's Favorite
★★★★★★★★★★★★★★ **Corn Bread** ★★★★★★★★★★★★★★

Submitted by Senator Charles E. Grassley

SERVES 6–8

*S*enator *Charles E. Grassley is a Republican and represents the state of Iowa.*

≡

lll

★

Charles E. Grassley

INGREDIENTS

¼ pound soft butter
1 cup sugar
2 eggs, beaten
1 cup cornmeal

1½ cups flour
2 teaspoons baking powder
¼ teaspoon salt
1½ cups milk

1. Preheat oven to 375°.
2. Cream butter and sugar. Stir in eggs and cornmeal.
3. Sift together flour, baking powder, and salt. Add to creamed mixture alternately with milk. Do not overbeat.
4. Put in a greased 8-inch square or 9 x 13 pan.
5. Bake for 35 minutes, or until a toothpick inserted in center of bread comes out clean.

★★★★★★★★★★★★ **Easy Corn Bread** ★★★★★★★★★★★★

Submitted by Representative Michael G. Oxley

SERVES 6–8

Congressman Michael G. Oxley is a Republican and represents the 4th District of Ohio.

INGREDIENTS

1 egg
1 cup buttermilk
¼ cup honey
1 cup yellow cornmeal
1 cup flour

2 teaspoons baking powder
½ teaspoon baking soda
½ teaspoon salt
3 tablespoons melted butter
Cheddar cheese

1. Preheat oven to 425°.
2. Beat together egg, buttermilk, and honey.
3. In a separate bowl, mix all dry ingredients.
4. Combine moist and dry ingredients. Add melted butter, and mix well.
5. Spread into a buttered 8-inch square pan and bake for 20 minutes.
6. Serve hot with butter and cheddar cheese.

✱✱✱✱✱✱✱ **Georgia Peach Bread Recipe** ✱✱✱✱✱✱✱✱

Submitted by Senator Sam Nunn
From the Kitchen of Colleen Nunn

SERVES 6–8 EACH LOAF   MAKES 2 LOAVES

Senator Sam Nunn is a Democrat and represents the state of Georgia.

113
✱

Sam Nunn

INGREDIENTS

3 cups sliced fresh peaches
6 tablespoons sugar
2 cups all-purpose flour
1 teaspoon baking soda
¼ teaspoon salt
1 teaspoon ground cinnamon

1½ cups sugar
½ cup shortening
2 eggs, beaten
1 cup finely chopped pecans
1 teaspoon vanilla

1. Preheat oven to 325°.
2. Place peaches and 6 tablespoons sugar in blender and process until pureed (mixture should yield about 2¼ cups).
3. Combine flour, baking soda, salt, and cinnamon; set aside.
4. Cream 1½ cups sugar and shortening. Add eggs and mix well. Add peach puree.
5. Add dry ingredients and stir until moistened.
6. Stir in nuts and vanilla.
7. Spoon batter into 2 well greased and floured 9 x 5 x 3 loaf pans. Bake for 55–60 minutes, or until done.
8. Cool 10 minutes in pan; then turn onto rack and cool completely.

★★★★★★★ Quick and Easy Banana Bread ★★★★★★★

Submitted by Senator John H. Chafee

SERVES 6–8

*S*enator John H. Chafee is a Republican and represents the state of Rhode Island.

INGREDIENTS

1¾ cups sifted flour
¾ teaspoon baking soda
1½ teaspoons cream of tartar
½ teaspoon salt

2 eggs
½ cup butter or shortening
2 small ripe bananas, sliced
¾ cup sugar

1. Preheat oven to 350°.
2. Sift flour, baking soda, cream of tartar, and salt into a mixing bowl.
3. Mix eggs, butter, bananas, and sugar in blender on high speed for 2–3 minutes.
4. Pour wet ingredients over dry ingredients and mix well.
5. Pour into greased 9 x 5 x 3 loaf pan and bake 45 minutes.
6. Cool in pan.

★★★★★★★★★★ **Swedish Rye Bread** ★★★★★★★★★★

Submitted by Representative Charles W. Stenholm
From the Kitchen of Cindy Stenholm

SERVES 6–8 EACH LOAF   MAKES 3 LOAVES

ongressman Charles W. Stenholm is a Democrat and represents the *17th* District of Texas.

INGREDIENTS

3 cups milk
3 tablespoons butter
1 cup molasses
2 ¼-ounce packages dry yeast
¼ cup lukewarm water

¼ cup plus 2 tablespoons sugar
1 tablespoon salt
2 cups rye flour
8 cups sifted white flour

1. Preheat oven to 325°.

2. Scald milk but do not boil. Add butter and molasses to milk and let it cool.

3. Mix yeast and lukewarm water. Add sugar and salt to yeast mixture. Add yeast mixture to cool milk.

4. Stir in rye flour and 6–8 cups sifted white flour.

5. Knead on floured board.

6. Let dough rise in a greased bowl until double in size. After it has risen, punch it down and form into 3 loaves.

7. Place dough in 9 x 5 x 3 loaf pans or 1-pound coffee cans that have been greased and floured, and let rise again.

8. Bake for 45 minutes, or until lightly browned.

9. Remove from pans and cool on rack.

May be frozen.

115

★

Charles W. Stenholm

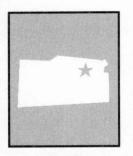

★★★★★★★★★★ Zucchini Nut Bread ★★★★★★★★★★★

Submitted by Representative Sam Brownback
From the Kitchen of Mary Brownback

SERVES 6–8 EACH LOAF   MAKES 2 LOAVES

Congressman Sam Brownback is a Republican and represents the 2nd District of Kansas.

INGREDIENTS

3 eggs, beaten
1 cup oil
2 cups sugar
2 cups grated zucchini
3 teaspoons vanilla
3 cups flour

1 teaspoon salt
½ teaspoon baking powder
1 teaspoon baking soda
3 teaspoons cinnamon
2 teaspoons nutmeg
1 cup chopped pecans

1. Preheat oven to 325°.
2. Mix together first 5 ingredients in a large bowl.
3. Sift flour and spices together, add to wet ingredients, and mix to combine. Sir in nuts.
4. Pour mixture into 2 greased and floured 9 x 5 x 3 loaf pans.
5. Bake about 1 hour.

Freezes well.

Pasta Dishes

★★★★★★★★★★★★ **Pizza Casserole** ★★★★★★★★★★★★

Submitted by Representative James B. Longley, Jr.
From the Kitchen of Mrs. James B. Longley

SERVES 6–8

Congressman James B. Longley, Jr., is a Republican and represents the 1st District of Maine.

★

James B. Longley Jr.

INGREDIENTS

⅓ cup butter or margarine

1 large onion, finely chopped (about 1½ cups)

2 8-ounce cans tomato sauce

¼ pound fresh mushrooms, sliced (about 1⅔ cups)

1 large clove garlic, minced

½ teaspoon dried oregano, crumbled

½ teaspoon dried basil, crumbled

1 8-ounce package spaghetti, cooked and drained

1 4-ounce package thinly sliced pepperoni

8 ounces mozzarella cheese, grated (about 2 cups)

3½ ounces Swiss cheese, grated (about 1 cup)

1. Preheat oven to 350°.

2. Melt butter in heavy skillet. Add onion and cook over medium-high heat until translucent, about 6 minutes. Remove from skillet with slotted spoon and set aside.

3. Combine tomato sauce, mushrooms, garlic, oregano, basil, and onion, and mix thoroughly.

4. Arrange spaghetti in bottom of lightly greased 9 x 13 baking dish. Top with half of tomato sauce mixture, dot with half of pepperoni, and sprinkle with half of cheeses.

5. Repeat layering with remaining tomato sauce mixture, pepperoni, and cheeses. (Can be prepared ahead to this point and refrigerated.)

6. Bake until heated through, about 25–30 minutes. Serve immediately.

★★★★★★★★★★★★ **Pasta Frittata** ★★★★★★★★★★★★

Submitted by Representative Pat Schroeder

SERVES 4

*C*ongresswoman Patricia Schroeder is a Democrat and represents the 1st District of Colorado.

INGREDIENTS

3 ounces vermicelli
4 eggs
3 tablespoons milk
1 tablespoon chopped fresh basil
Salt to taste
¼ teaspoon freshly ground black pepper
1 small onion, finely chopped

¼ cup plus 2 tablespoons chopped fresh
   parsley
1 clove garlic, crushed
¼ cup butter or margarine
1¼ cups shredded Swiss or cheddar
   cheese

1. Cook vermicelli according to package directions, omitting salt. Drain and set aside.

2. Combine eggs, milk, basil, salt, and pepper; beat well. Stir in vermicelli and set aside.

3. Sauté onion, ¼ cup parsley, and garlic in butter in a 10-inch nonstick skillet; remove from heat.

4. Stir in vermicelli mixture; sprinkle with cheese, and the remaining parsley if desired.

5. Cover and cook over low heat 5–7 minutes, or until cheese melts and egg mixture is set.

6. Let stand 5 minutes before serving. Cut in wedges.

120
★
Pasta Dishes

Submitted by Senator Alfonse D'Amato
From the Kitchen of Antoinette D'Amato

Alfonse D'Amato

SERVES 6–8

*S*enator Alfonse D'Amato is a Republican and represents the state of New York.

Preparation Tip: You may want to use your favorite tomato sauce instead of the one given. If you do, add a little water to the mixture.

INGREDIENTS

1 pound ricotta cheese
1 egg, beaten
¼ cup chopped fresh parsley
Salt and freshly ground pepper to taste
¼ cup Romano cheese
1 pound Italian sausage, sliced
1 pound lean ground beef
1 pound lasagna noodles
¼ pound mozzarella cheese, thinly sliced

Homemade Tomato Sauce:

3 cloves garlic
¼ onion, chopped fine
Olive oil
4 pounds Italian plum tomatoes, peeled
   and chopped

1. To prepare sauce, sauté garlic and onion in olive oil in a medium saucepan. When onion becomes translucent, discard garlic and add tomatoes. Simmer for 45 minutes.
2. Preheat oven to 400°.
3. Combine ricotta cheese, egg, parsley, salt, pepper, and Romano cheese.
4. Brown Italian sausage with ground beef.
5. Cook lasagna noodles until they are *al denté*.
6. Cover bottom of a 9½ x 13½ baking dish with lasagna noodles. Layer with ricotta mixture, cover with a layer of mozzarella cheese, and add tomato sauce on top.
7. Add a layer of beef and sausage combination.
8. Continue adding layers until pan is full. Spread sauce on as final layer.
9. Bake for 30 minutes.
10. When the lasagna is finished, let it set for a few minutes before serving.

★★★ Sherry's Spaghetti Sauce and Meatballs ★★★

Submitted by Representative Sherwood Boehlert

SERVES 6–8   ENOUGH FOR 2 POUNDS SPAGHETTI

66 *ne of my favorite recipes. . . ."*
—*Congressman Sherwood Boehlert is a Republican and represents the 23rd District of New York.*

MEATBALL INGREDIENTS

1 pound lean ground beef
2 eggs
1 teaspoon salt
Garlic salt to taste
¼ cup bread crumbs
2 tablespoons Romano cheese
1 teaspoon black pepper
1 tablespoon dried parsley

Sauce:

1½ pounds Italian sausage
1 28-ounce can tomato puree
1 6-ounce can tomato paste
2 teaspoons dried oregano
1 teaspoon salt
½ 28-ounce can water
1–2 teaspoons sugar
2 bay leaves
2 cloves garlic, chopped
1 teaspoon dried basil
3 tablespoons oil from cooking meatballs

1. Fry sausage until brown. Drain on paper towel, then slice. Save sausage oil to brown meatballs in.

2. Mix all ingredients for meatballs; shape and brown in sausage oil (there should be 4–5 tablespoons oil), turning frequently.

3. Combine all sauce ingredients in large pot.

4. Add meatballs and sausage to sauce and simmer for at least 3 hours.

★★★★★★★★★★ **Extra-Meaty Lasagna** ★★★★★★★★★★

Submitted by Senator Kent Conrad
From the Kitchen of Lucy Calautti

SERVES 10

❝ *This is a great main meal just for the family or for dinner guests. The only other dish you need with this is a tossed salad to make a complete meal. I use prepared tomato sauce because it's so good and saves time.*❞
—*Lucy Calautti, wife of Senator Kent Conrad. Senator Conrad is a Democrat and represents the state of North Dakota.*

Preparation Tip: This recipe can be prepared in advance and refrigerated. If assembled in advance, bake for 45 minutes to 1 hour.

INGREDIENTS

1½ pounds extra-lean ground beef	*Dash of salt*
1 medium onion, chopped	*¼ cup vegetable or olive oil*
1 pound sweet Italian sausage links	*8 ounces lasagna noodles*
1 16-ounce jar seasoned meaty tomato	*3 cups low-fat cottage cheese*
* sauce*	*2 tablespoons dried parsley flakes*
1 teaspoon dried oregano	*1 egg, beaten*
1 teaspoon ground black pepper	*1 pound mozzarella cheese, shredded*
1 teaspoon garlic powder	*1 cup grated Parmesan cheese*

1. Preheat oven to 375°.

2. Brown ground beef and onions. Add a small amount of oil to moisten, if necessary. Remove from pan.

3. Retain fat in pan and add sausage links. Brown on all sides.

4. In saucepan, place tomato sauce, oregano, pepper, and garlic powder. Add ground beef and onion. Mix all ingredients and simmer.

5. Drain fat from sausage, patting sausage with paper towel to remove excess fat and oil. Place sausage in saucepan with tomato sauce and meat mixture, and continue simmering. Do not boil. Stir often.

123
★

Kent Conrad

6. Meanwhile, bring water, salt, and oil to boil in a large pot. Add noodles, one at a time. Bring to second boil, and cook according to directions on lasagna package.

7. While noodles are cooking, mix cottage cheese, parsley, and egg in a bowl. Set aside.

8. Stir sauce to avoid sticking. After sauce has cooked for 15 minutes (or when sausage is cooked through), remove from heat.

9. Remove sausage from sauce and cut into ¼-inch round slices.

10. Drain noodles. Layer half the noodles in a lightly greased 13 x 9 x 2 baking dish; spread with half the cottage cheese mixture; add half the sausage slices, half the sauce and meat mixture; sprinkle with half the shredded mozzarella cheese.

11. Repeat layers. Sprinkle Parmesan cheese on top.

12. Bake for 30–35 minutes, or until heated through.

13. Wait a few minutes after baking, then slice portions and serve.

124

★

Pasta Dishes

Soups and Chowders

★★★★★★★★★★ **Instant Meatball Soup** ★★★★★★★★★★

Submitted by Senator Alfonse D'Amato
From the Kitchen of Antoinette D'Amato

SERVES 2–3

66 *Over the years, I have discovered that many of my family's favorite dishes are not only easy to prepare and nutritious, but also economical. I hope you enjoy this collection* of our favorites."*
—Antoinette D'Amato, mother of Senator Alfonse D'Amato. Senator D'Amato is a Republican and represents the state of New York.

Preparation Tip: Boiled pasta or rice may be added to this soup before serving.

INGREDIENTS

4 cups water
2 large carrots, peeled and cubed
3 large celery stalks, diced
1 medium-sized onion, diced
4 chicken bouillon cubes

½ pound lean ground beef
Salt and pepper to taste
½ cup grated Romano or Parmesan
cheese

1. Boil water in a large saucepan or soup kettle. Add carrots, celery, and onion. Cover and cook until vegetables are tender.
2. Add bouillon cubes and simmer.
3. Season ground beef with salt and pepper and shape into tiny meatballs (½-inch diameter).
4. Add meatballs to soup, and cook 3–5 minutes.
5. Serve with grated cheese.

127
★
Alfonse D'Amato

*Other recipes from the D'Amato family appear on pages 44, 61, 89, 102, 121, and 128.

★★★★★★★★★★★★★★ **Lentil Soup** ★★★★★★★★★★★★★★★

Submitted by Senator Alfonse D'Amato
From the Kitchen of Antoinette D'Amato

SERVES 3

$\mathcal{S}$enator Alfonse D'Amato is a Republican and represents the state of New York.

Preparation Tip: Small boiled pasta (macaroni) may be added to soup before serving.

INGREDIENTS

1 cup lentils
4 slices bacon, cut in small pieces
1 clove garlic
3 tablespoons tomato sauce

2 cups water
1 tablespoon chopped fresh parsley
Salt and ground pepper to taste

1. Wash lentils under cold water. Drain.

2. Sauté bacon in large saucepan with garlic until garlic is golden brown. Remove garlic.

3. Stir in tomato sauce. Add water. Let soup base cook to a rolling boil.

4. Add lentils to base. Cook 30–45 minutes, over medium heat, adding more water as needed during cooking.

5. When lentils are tender, add parsley and salt and pepper to taste.

★★★★★★★★ **Charleston She-Crab Soup** ★★★★★★★★

Submitted by Senator Ernest F. Hollings

SERVES 4–6

Senator Ernest F. Hollings is a Democrat and represents the state of South Carolina.

INGREDIENTS

2 tablespoons butter
2 teaspoons flour
2 cups whole milk
½ cup cream
½ teaspoon mace
¼ teaspoon celery salt

1 tablespoon Worcestershire sauce
1 pound lump crabmeat, with roe if
    possible
Salt and pepper to taste
Sherry, warmed in pitcher

1. Melt butter in top of double boiler and blend in flour until smooth. Add milk, then cream, very slowly.
2. To this add mace, celery salt, and Worcestershire sauce.
3. Add the crabmeat and fold in gently.
4. Add salt and pepper.
5. Ladle soup into individual serving bowls.
6. Add sherry to taste to each bowl.

★

Ernest F. Hollings

The Famous Senate Restaurant
★★★★★★★★★★★★★★★★ **Bean Soup** ★★★★★★★★★★★★★★★★

Submitted by Senator Carl Levin

SERVES 8

*H*istory of Senate Bean Soup: *"Whatever uncertainties may exist in the Senate of the United States, one thing is sure: Bean Soup is on the menu of the Senate Restaurant every day. The origin of the culinary decree has been lost in antiquity, but there are several oft-repeated legends. One story has it that Senator Fred Thomas Dubois of Idaho, who served in the Senate from 1901 to 1907, when chairman of the committee that supervised the Senate Restaurant, gaveled through a resolution requiring that Bean Soup be on the menu every day. Another account attributes the Bean Soup Mandate to Senator Knute Nelson of Minnesota, who expressed his fondness for it in 1902. In any case, senators and their guests are always assured of a hearty, nourishing dish; they know they can rely upon its delightful flavor and epicurean qualities."*

—Senator Carl Levin is a Democrat and represents the state of Michigan.

INGREDIENTS

2 pounds small Michigan navy beans	1 onion, chopped
4 quarts hot water	Butter
1½ pounds smoked ham hocks	Salt and pepper to taste

1. Wash beans by running through hot water until the beans are white again. Soak beans according to package directions, then drain.

2. Put beans and water in a large soup pot and bring to a boil.

3. Add ham hocks, cover pot, and boil slowly until beans are tender, approximately 3 hours.

4. Remove ham hocks from soup. Cut meat off bones and discard bones. Mince meat and return to soup.

5. Braise onion in a little butter, and when light brown, add to soup.

6. Do not add salt until ready to serve; then season to taste with salt and pepper.

★★★★★★★★★★★★★ **Squash Soup** ★★★★★★★★★★★★★★

Submitted by Representative Steve Stockman
From the Kitchen of Dee Vordenbaum

★

Steve Stockman

SERVES 4

66 *This is one of my favorite meals. This very sweet woman cooked for us during the campaign."*
—*Congressman Steve Stockman is a Republican and represents the 9th District of Texas.*

INGREDIENTS

¼ *pound pepper bacon, chopped*
8 medium yellow squash, sliced
1 medium onion, chopped

5 ounces sharp cheddar cheese, grated
Salt (optional)

1. If possible, precook bacon in microwave oven, thus removing fat; chop.

2. Place squash, bacon, and onion in pot with less water than to cover.

3. Cook at medium heat for 45 minutes if bacon is not precooked, or 30 minutes if bacon is precooked.

4. Place in blender (5 cup capacity) 4 cups squash and liquid and half the cheese.

5. Blend, and fill first 2 soup bowls.

6. Blend remaining ingredients with remaining cheese, and fill last 2 soup bowls.

7. Since bacon has salt, taste before salting; add more salt if needed.

★★★★★★★★★★★ **Missouri Apple Soup** ★★★★★★★★★★★

Submitted by Senator Christopher Bond
From the Kitchen of Caroline Bond

SERVES 10–12

66 *Stephenson's Apple Orchard in Eastern Jackson County is a name that brings to mind family outings during the fall picking season and bushel baskets heaping with succulent apples. Why not reserve a few Jonathans for this unusual soup?"*

—*Senator Christopher Bond is a Republican and represents the state of Missouri.*

INGREDIENTS

2 tablespoons butter

2 medium onions, thinly sliced

6 red Jonathan apples, peeled, cored, and diced

4 cups chicken broth

2 tablespoons sugar

1 tablespoon curry powder, or to taste

Salt and freshly ground white pepper to taste

1–2 cups light cream, or to taste

Sliced almonds and thin apple wedges to garnish

1. In a Dutch oven, melt butter and sauté onions until transparent.
2. Add apples, broth, sugar, and curry powder. Season with salt and pepper.
3. Cook covered over low heat until apples are soft, approximately 30 minutes.
4. Strain apples and onions from broth and reserve; set broth aside.
5. Place apples and onions in food processor or blender and puree.
6. Add broth and blend well.
7. Add cream according to desired richness; chill.
8. Taste and adjust seasonings.
9. Serve cold, garnished with thin apple wedges and a sprinkling of sliced almonds.

★★★★★★★★★★★ **Potato-Dill Soup** ★★★★★★★★★★★★

Submitted by Senator Daniel Patrick Moynihan

SERVES 6–8

*S*enator Daniel Patrick Moynihan is a Democrat and represents the state of New York.

INGREDIENTS

7 large potatoes, peeled
2 onions, chopped
1 bunch green onions, chopped
Large amount chopped fresh dill (1–2
*   teaspoons, or to taste; reserve some for*
*   garnish)*

2 tablespoons butter
1 pint heavy cream
2 cups sour cream
Salt to taste
Freshly ground pepper to taste
Parsley sprigs for garnish

1. Cook potatoes with onions in boiling water until they begin to fall apart. Strain.
2. Add scallions, dill, butter, and heavy cream, and cook for 10 minutes.
3. Stir in 1 cup sour cream and heat through for 2 minutes. Add salt to taste.
4. Garnish each bowl with pepper, dill, parsley, and 1 tablespoon sour cream.

153
★

Daniel Patrick Moynihan

★★★★★★★★★★ **Chicken Velvet Soup** ★★★★★★★★★★★★

Submitted by Representative George R. Nethercutt, Jr.

SERVES 6–8

66 *It is a pleasure to share two of my family's favorite recipes."* *
*—Congressman George R. Nethercutt, Jr., is a Republican and represents
the 5th District of Washington.*

INGREDIENTS

1½ sticks butter or margarine
¾ cup flour
1 cup milk (nonfat is fine)
1 cup half-and-half
6 cups chicken broth
*2 cups finely chopped cooked chicken
    breast*

1 cup finely chopped celery (optional)
Salt and pepper to taste
1 teaspoon dried tarragon (optional)
*Chopped fresh parsley for garnish
    (optional)*

1. Melt butter and whisk in flour to make a roux. Cook for 2 minutes.

2. Heat milk, half-and-half, and broth together and add a little at a time to roux until mixture thickens. Whisk until smooth.

3. When soup starts to boil, add chicken, celery, and seasonings.

4. You may omit tarragon and garnish with fresh chopped parsley if you prefer.

*Congressman Nethercutt's second recipe appears on page 99.

★★★★★★★★★★★ Dale's Crab Soup ★★★★★★★★★★★

Submitted by Senator Dale Bumpers

SERVES 6–8

*S*enator Dale Bumpers is a Democrat and represents the state of Arkansas.

★

Dale Bumpers

Preparation Tip: The amounts in this recipe are for 1 pound of crabmeat. Use lump, or backfin, crab if you can get it. It will have small pieces of shell in it, so you will have to pick it over carefully. If lump crabmeat is not available, canned crabmeat will do.

INGREDIENTS

1 large stalk celery, finely chopped
1 large onion, finely chopped
³⁄₄–1 stick butter
2 quarts milk
1 pint half-and-half

1 pound lump (backfin) crab
1 clove garlic, minced
Salt and pepper to taste
Hot pepper sauce
Oyster crackers or croutons

1. Sauté celery and onion in ½ stick butter until very soft.

2. In a separate pan, heat milk and half-and-half together.

3. Add cooked onion and celery, crab, garlic, and about ¼ stick butter (or more, according to taste).

4. Season with salt, pepper, and hot pepper sauce according to taste.

5. Heat thoroughly and serve with oyster crackers or croutons.

★★★★★★★★★★★★★★ **Grape Soup** ★★★★★★★★★★★★★★★

Submitted by Representative John W. Olver
From the Kitchen of Helen Fulleborn Olver

SERVES 4

❝*The following is an old family recipe dating back to my mother's Central European, German origins. Mother, Helen Fulleborn Olver, is now eighty-eight years old. I like this soup because it is tart and thick like other European cold and hot fruit soups.*❞
—*Congressman John W. Olver is a Democrat and represents the 1st District of Massachusetts.*

INGREDIENTS
2 tablespoons butter
1½ tablespoons flour
3 cups hot grape juice
¼ cup sugar
Pinch of salt
1 stick cinnamon
10–12 cloves
Croutons

Juice:
1 quart Concord grapes, washed, stems
 removed
1⅓ cups water

Croutons:
2 tablespoons butter
2–3 slices white bread, cut into small
 cubes

To Make Juice:

1. Place grapes and water in large pot, bring to boil, and simmer for about 10 minutes.
2. Strain through coarse sieve or put through a ricer or food mill (grape pulp in the juice is good for the soup).

To Make Soup:

1. Melt butter in a large pot over low heat.
2. Add flour, stirring constantly. Continue to stir while slowly adding 3 cups hot grape juice.

3. Add sugar and season with salt, cinnamon stick, and cloves.

4. Serve hot, with croutons sprinkled on top.

To Make Croutons:

1. Melt butter in medium skillet.

2. Brown cubes over medium heat, stirring constantly. (Can be prepared ahead.)

★

John W. Olver

138

★

Soups and Chowders

★★★★★★★★★★★★★ **Clam Chowder** ★★★★★★★★★★★★★

Submitted by Senator John H. Chafee

SERVES 8–10

❝*These particular culinary delights are representative of some of the many tastes of my fellow Rhode Islanders. . . .* As you know, Rhode Island's nickname is the Ocean State, and the fishing industry is one of the major commercial sectors of our economy. Shucked clams and quahogs are enjoyed by many of our citizens, and clam chowder is a preferred seafood dish of many Rhode Islanders as well.*❞
—*Senator John H. Chafee is a Republican and represents the state of Rhode Island.*

Preparation Tip: The flavor of this soup gets even better as it stands and seasons.

INGREDIENTS

1 quart shucked clams or quahogs
⅓ cup diced salt pork
1 tablespoon butter
1 onion, diced
3 cups water

4 cups finely diced potatoes
2 cups milk
1 small can evaporated milk
1 cup light cream

1. Remove hard neck of clams and discard. Chop clams coarsely.

2. Fry salt pork in butter in a large saucepan, remove pieces of pork.

3. Add onion and cook until clear.

4. Add water and potatoes. Cook 3–4 minutes.

5. Add clams and cook until potatoes are soft but not falling apart, approximately 30 minutes.

6. Add milk and cream.

7. Season to taste with salt and pepper.

*Other Rhode Island recipes from Senator Chafee appear on pages 114 and 145.

✶✶✶✶✶✶✶✶ **Rhode Island Clam Chowder** ✶✶✶✶✶✶✶✶

Submitted by Senator Claiborne Pell

SERVES 4

*S*enator Claiborne Pell is a Democrat and represents the state of Rhode Island.

INGREDIENTS

⅛ pound fat salt pork, chopped
4–5 large onions, chopped
1 pint shucked clams, separated and chopped (water reserved)
1 quart water

3–4 large potatoes
Salt and pepper to taste
2 tablespoons butter (more if your conscience will let you)
1 tablespoon sugar (optional)

1. Fry salt pork. Remove pork and fry onions in pork fat.

2. Place chopped clam necks and water from same together with chopped salt pork and onions in kettle with water. Let boil while preparing potatoes.

2. Peel potatoes and dice into ½-inch pieces. Put into kettle. Bring to a boil, then simmer for 30–45 minutes over moderate heat to prevent sticking.

3. Add a good deal of salt and pepper to taste.

4. When potatoes are soft, add remaining parts of clams and butter.

5. Bring to a boil again, then simmer over moderate heat another 3 minutes.

6. Add sugar if you like.

Claiborne Pell

★★★★★★★★ **Easy Hearty Corn Chowder** ★★★★★★★★

Submitted by Senator Kay Bailey Hutchison

SERVES 4–6

*S*enator Kay Bailey Hutchison is a Republican and represents the state of Texas.

INGREDIENTS

1 15-ounce can creamed corn
1 15-ounce can whole-kernel corn
1 10¾-ounce can cream of chicken soup
1 raw potato, chopped in small pieces

¾ cup chopped celery
½ cup cooked and chopped bacon,
* sausage, or ham*
Salt and pepper to taste

1. Blend all ingredients and cook over low heat until potatoes and celery are tender, approximately 30–45 minutes.
2. Add water for desired thickness.

★★★ Ted Kennedy's Cape Cod Fish Chowder ★★★

Submitted by Senator Ted Kennedy

SERVES 8

*S*enator Ted Kennedy is a Democrat and represents the state of Massachusetts.

141
★
Ted Kennedy

INGREDIENTS

2 pounds fresh haddock
2 cups water
2 ounces salt pork, diced
2 medium onions, sliced
1 cup chopped celery

4 large potatoes, diced
1 bay leaf, crumbled
4 cups milk
2 tablespoons butter or margarine
Salt and freshly ground pepper to taste

1. Simmer haddock in water for 15 minutes. Drain off and reserve broth.
2. Remove skin and bones from fish.
3. Sauté diced salt pork in a large pot until crisp.
4. Remove salt pork and sauté onions in pork fat until golden brown.
5. Add fish, celery, potatoes, and bay leaf.
6. Measure reserved fish broth, and add enough boiling water to make 3 cups liquid.
7. Add to pot and simmer 40 minutes.
8. Add milk and butter and simmer for an additional 5 minutes, or until well heated.
9. Season with salt and pepper.

Brunch Dishes

★★★★ Aunt Evelyn's Johnnycake or Muffins ★★★★

Submitted by Senator John H. Chafee

SERVES 6–8

*S*enator John H. Chafee is a Republican and represents the state of Rhode Island.

INGREDIENTS

1½ cups cornmeal
½ cup flour
¼ cup sugar
1 teaspoon salt
¾ teaspoon baking soda
1½ teaspoons baking powder

1 egg, beaten
1¼ cups sour milk (milk with 1
*   tablespoon lemon juice or vinegar*
*   added)*
3 tablespoons butter, melted

1. Preheat oven to 425°.
2. Mix and sift dry ingredients into a mixing bowl.
3. Combine beaten egg, sour milk, and melted butter. Add to dry mixture.
4. Stir lightly and pour into a greased 9 x 9 baking pan or muffin tins.
5. Bake 25 minutes.

145
★

John H. Chafee

★★★★★★★★★★★ **Swedish Pancakes** ★★★★★★★★★★★★

Submitted by Senator Patty Murray

SERVES 4

Senator Patty Murray is a Democrat and represents the state of Washington.

INGREDIENTS

1½ cups flour
1 scant teaspoon salt
3 teaspoons sugar
3 large eggs, or 4 small eggs
2 cups milk

1 tablespoon butter, melted
Freshly squeezed lemon juice
Powdered sugar
Fresh strawberries, or other fresh fruit

1. Combine flour, salt, and sugar in a bowl.
2. Whip eggs and milk together, then blend slowly into dry mixture. Add melted butter.

For One Large Pancake:

1. Preheat oven to 350°.
2. Pour batter into a greased 12-inch cast iron skillet and bake until brown.
3. Serve sprinkled with lemon juice, powdered sugar, and fresh fruit such as strawberries.

For Individual Pancakes:

1. Use a scant ½ cup batter per pancake and fry in a greased skillet.
2. These will be very thin and can be rolled. They can be sprinkled with lemon juice and powdered sugar, and served with fresh fruit.

★★★★★★★ **Dentist's Dream French Toast** ★★★★★★★

Submitted by Representative Joseph P. Kennedy II

SERVES 2–3

Congressman Joseph P. Kennedy II is a Democrat and represents the 8th District of Massachusetts.

INGREDIENTS

5 large eggs
¼ cup heavy cream
1 tablespoon sugar
¼ teaspoon cinnamon

1 capful vanilla
4 tablespoons butter, or more as needed
6 slices white bread
Powdered sugar

1. Combine eggs, cream, sugar, cinnamon, and vanilla in a bowl.
2. Melt butter in a large frying pan as needed.
3. Soak slices of bread in egg mixture and fry on each side until lightly browned.
4. Sprinkle lightly with powdered sugar if desired, and dig in—then call the dentist!

147
★

Joseph P. Kennedy II

★★★★★★★★★★ **Mom's English Scones** ★★★★★★★★★★

Submitted by Senator James Inhofe

MAKES APPROXIMATELY 12–14 SCONES

enator James Inhofe is a Republican and represents the state of Oklahoma.

Preparation Tip: Instant buttermilk, now available, is a quick way to make this recipe even easier. You may also use raisins in place of currants. Use a doughnut round without the center to cut out the scones. Delicious while hot with whipped butter.

INGREDIENTS

2 cups flour

¼ cup white sugar

½ teaspoon salt

2½ teaspoons baking powder

½ teaspoon baking soda

¼ cup shortening

¼ cup currants

1 cup buttermilk

1. Preheat oven to 450°.

2. Sift dry ingredients into a bowl and cut in shortening.

3. Add currants and buttermilk (dough will be sticky).

4. Knead 1 minute on floured surface and cut into rounds.

5. Place on ungreased cookie sheet and bake for 12–15 minutes.

★★★★★★★★★★ **Giant Apple Popovers** ★★★★★★★★★★

Submitted by Senator Arlen Specter

SERVES 8–10

*S*enator Arlen Specter is a Republican and represents the state of Pennsylvania.

★

Arlen Specter

INGREDIENTS

6 eggs
1½ cups flour
½ teaspoon salt
1 tablespoon sugar
1½ cups milk
¾ cup butter

3 large apples, peeled, cored, and thinly sliced
Freshly squeezed lemon juice
¾ cup sugar
2 tablespoons cinnamon

1. Preheat oven to 425°.
2. Beat eggs, stir in flour, salt, and 1 tablespoon sugar until smooth; gradually stir in milk. Set batter aside. (Batter may be made ahead.)
3. Divide butter between 2 heavy 9-inch skillets. If handles are not ovenproof, wrap them with foil to protect from heat.
4. Sprinkle apple slices with lemon juice and divide between pans.
5. Divide sugar and cinnamon over apples and sauté until glazed and golden. (Apples may be prepared ahead.)
6. Divide batter into pans and put pans in oven.
7. Bake 20–25 minutes, until puffed and golden brown. Serve at once.

Appetizers and Dips

★★★★★★★★★ **Miniature Ham Rolls** ★★★★★★★★★

Submitted by Senator Strom Thurmond

SERVES 10–12

enator Strom Thurmond is a Republican and represents the state of South Carolina.

153
★
Strom Thurmond

INGREDIENTS

2 packages small tea rolls
  (approximately 12)
8 ounces sliced ham, each slice cut into
  fourths
6 ounces sliced Swiss cheese, each slice
  cut into fourths

1½ teaspoons poppy seeds
½ teaspoon Worcestershire sauce
1½ tablespoons prepared mustard
1 tablespoon onion flakes

1. Preheat oven to 350°.

2. Slice rolls lengthwise through center. Put ham and cheese on bottom. Put roll top back on. Place in baking pan.

3. Mix remaining ingredients and spread over top.

4. Place in greased baking pan, cover with aluminum foil, and bake for 15 minutes.

★★★★★★★★★★★★★★ **Josefinas** ★★★★★★★★★★★★★★

Submitted by Representative John T. Myers

MAKES 5 DOZEN

*C*ongressman John T. Myers is a Republican and represents the 7th District of Indiana.

INGREDIENTS

1 loaf firm white sandwich bread, crusts
on, each slice quartered
½ pound soft butter or margarine
1 cup chopped canned green chilies (use
less if fresh)

1 clove garlic, crushed
½ pound shredded cheddar cheese
1 cup mayonnaise

1. Preheat broiler.
2. Mix chilies and garlic into butter and spread bread with mixture.
3. Combine cheese and mayonnaise and spread over top.
4. Broil until brown and fluffy, approximately 2–4 minutes.

★★★★★★★★★★★★ **Cheese Straws** ★★★★★★★★★★★★

Submitted by Senator Howell Heflin
From the Kitchen of Mrs. Howell Heflin

SERVES 6–8

S enator Howell Heflin is a Democrat and represents the state of Alabama.

Preparation Tip: You can find a cheese straw press at any fine kitchen supply store. If you don't have a cheese straw press, simply roll dough to straw thickness and cut into 4-inch logs.

155
★
Howell Heflin

INGREDIENTS

1 pound sharp cheddar cheese, grated, at
room temperature
1 stick butter or margarine, at room
temperature

2 cups sifted flour
½ teaspoon salt
¼ teaspoon cayenne pepper
¼ teaspoon paprika

1. Preheat oven to 350°.
2. Combine cheese and butter, and mix well.
3. Add dry ingredients, and mix well.
4. Put through cheese straw press onto ungreased cookie sheets.
5. Cut into 4-inch pieces before cooking, or break after cooking.
6. Bake about 15 minutes, or until dried out but not brown.

★★★★★★ **Hot Chicken Wings à la Thomas** ★★★★★★

Submitted by Senator Craig Thomas
From the Kitchen of Mrs. Craig Thomas

SERVES 3–4

*S*enator Craig Thomas is a Republican and represents the state of Wyoming.

INGREDIENTS
1 pound chicken wings
½ stick butter (less will do)
1–2 4-ounce bottles hot sauce

1. Preheat oven to 400°.
2. Cut off and discard flippers from wings.
3. Put wings on rack of broiler pan and roast for 30 minutes. Turn and cook another 30 minutes.
4. Meanwhile, melt butter over low heat in a saucepan.
5. Add hot sauce. Heat until mixed.
6. After wings are cooked (should be crispy), put into hot sauce and mix to coat thoroughly.
7. Right before serving, put wings on broiler pan and broil for 30 seconds to crisp topping.
8. Get lots of napkins and water! Enjoy.

★★★★★★★★★★★ **Tostada Grande** ★★★★★★★★★★★

Submitted by Representative John T. Myers

SERVES 16

*C*ongressman John T. Myers is a Republican and represents the 7th District of Indiana.

INGREDIENTS

3 medium-size ripe avocados
2 tablespoons lemon juice
½ teaspoon salt
¼ teaspoon pepper
1 cup (8 ounces) sour cream
½ cup mayonnaise
1 1¼-ounce package taco seasoning mix
2 10½-ounce cans plain or jalapeno bean dip

2 cups chopped green onions, including tops
1 cup seeded and chopped tomatoes
2 3½-ounce cans pitted ripe olives, chopped and drained
8 ounces sharp cheddar cheese, shredded
Large, round tortilla chips
Green chilies (optional)

1. Peel, pit, and mash avocados. Mix in lemon juice, salt, and pepper.

2. Combine sour cream, mayonnaise, and taco mix in a separate bowl.

3. Spread bean dip in shallow 9-inch bowl for first layer. Spread avocado mixture on top of bean dip for second layer. Spread sour cream mixture on top for third layer. Add chopped onions for fourth layer. Add chopped tomatoes for fifth layer, chopped olives for sixth layer, and shredded cheese for top layer.

4. Serve chilled or at room temperature with tortilla chips.

5. If you prefer a hotter combination, add a layer of chopped green chilies or mix chilies with avocado mixture.

157
★
John T. Myers

✦✦✦✦✦✦✦✦✦✦ Hot Crab-Artichoke Dip ✦✦✦✦✦✦✦✦✦✦

Submitted by Representative John T. Myers
From the Kitchen of Sallie Davis

SERVES 6–8

Congressman John T. Myers is a Republican and represents the 7th District of Indiana.

INGREDIENTS

1 6½-ounce can lump crabmeat
1 14-ounce can artichoke hearts, drained and quartered
1 cup mayonnaise

2 3-ounce packages grated Parmesan cheese
Garlic salt to taste

1. Preheat oven to 350°.
2. Mix all ingredients together and place in casserole dish.
3. Bake uncovered for 30 minutes.
4. Serve hot with crackers.

★★★★★★★★★★★★ **Garbanzo Dip** ★★★★★★★★★★★★

Submitted by Senator Sam Nunn
From the Kitchen of Colleen Nunn

SERVES 6–8

159
★

Sam Nunn

Senator Sam Nunn is a Democrat and represents the state of Georgia.

Preparation Tip: Healthy as a dip for raw vegetables or as a spread with pita bread. This dip has only 35 calories per serving (approximately 1 tablespoon).

INGREDIENTS

1 20-ounce can garbanzo beans
   (chickpeas), drained
1 tablespoon olive oil
½ teaspoon sesame seeds

Freshly ground pepper
1 large clove garlic, minced
3 tablespoons freshly squeezed lemon juice
Fresh parsley, chopped

1. Combine all ingredients except parsley in blender until creamy. Chill.
2. Serve cold, sprinkled with chopped parsley.

★★★★★★★★★★★★★★★ Hot Crab Dip ★★★★★★★★★★★★★★★

Submitted by Representative John T. Myers
From the Kitchen of Sallie Davis

SERVES 10–12

*C*ongressman John T. Myers is a Republican and represents the 7th District of Indiana.

INGREDIENTS

3 8-ounce packages cream cheese

3 6½-ounce cans crabmeat, or 1¼ pounds
    lump (backfin) crabmeat

Dash of garlic salt

½ cup mayonnaise

2 teaspoons French's mustard

¼ cup white wine

2 teaspoons onion juice (optional)

2 teaspoons powdered sugar

Dash of seasoning salt

Dash of cayenne pepper

1. Melt cream cheese in top of double boiler.
2. Add remaining ingredients and combine well.
3. Serve hot with crackers.

Freezes well.

Miscellaneous

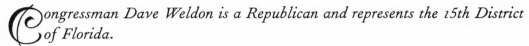# ★★★★★★★★ **Liz Bryant's Coffee Punch** ★★★★★★★★

Submitted by Representative Dave Weldon
From the Kitchen of Nancy Weldon

SERVES 15–20

Congressman Dave Weldon is a Republican and represents the 15th District of Florida.

163
★
Dave Weldon

INGREDIENTS

3 tablespoons instant coffee
1 cup boiling water
1 cup sugar

½ gallon chocolate ice cream (softened)
½ gallon vanilla ice cream (softened)
1 gallon milk

1. Combine coffee, water, and sugar in saucepan. Stir over medium heat for 8 minutes. Do not boil.

2. Chill until ready to serve.

3. Combine all ingredients in a chilled punch bowl, breaking up ice cream somewhat before adding milk.

4. Stir to get a more creamy consistency, then serve.

★★★★★★★★★★ **Indian Green Chutney** ★★★★★★★★★★★

Submitted by Senator Arlen Specter

SERVES 6–8

Senator Arlen Specter is a Republican and represents the state of Pennsyl-vania.

Preparation Tip: This works best in a food processor, and with great difficulty in a blender.

INGREDIENTS

2–3 hot green chili peppers, seeds
   removed
1 small piece fresh ginger, peeled
½ cup unsalted peanuts
3 tablespoons brown sugar (or Indian
   jaggery)
3 tablespoons coconut flakes
2 tablespoons sesame seeds
1 tablespoon coriander

1 tablespoon ground cumin
½ teaspoon hing (asafoetida powder;
   optional)
½ tablespoon turmeric
2 teaspoons cumin seed
2 tablespoons freshly squeezed lemon juice
   (or mango powder)
2 bunches fresh parsley, stems removed
1 bunch green onions, with some green

1. Place all the dry ingredients including chilies and ginger in a food processor or blender, and blend very well.

2. Add the lemon juice and greens and blend until very smooth.

3. Taste, and add more lemon, brown sugar, and green chilies as desired.

★★★★★★★★★★★ **Sesame Dressing** ★★★★★★★★★★★

Submitted by Representative John T. Myers

SERVES 4–6

*C*ongressman *John T. Myers is a Republican and represents the 7th District of Indiana.*

INGREDIENTS

1 cup corn oil (or other light vegetable oil)
⅓ cup soy sauce (preferably Japanese)
¼ cup freshly squeezed lemon juice

2–4 cloves garlic
½ onion, finely chopped (if strong, use less)
¼–½ cup sesame seeds

1. Preheat oven to 300°.

2. In a blender, mix first 5 ingredients and blend until thick and smooth. Transfer to a bowl or jar.

3. In a dry skillet or pan in the oven, toast sesame seeds until they begin to brown. Add warm seeds to dressing.

4. Taste, and add more lemon juice or soy sauce as needed to balance flavor.

5. Serve over your favorite salad greens.

★★★★★★★★★★★★★ **Crème Fraîche** ★★★★★★★★★★★★★

Submitted by Senator James Inhofe
From the Kitchen of Kay Inhofe

SERVES 6–8

Senator James Inhofe is a Republican and represents the state of Oklahoma.

Preparation Tip: This is great to spoon over fresh fruit, add to sauces, or simply spread over warm buttered vegetables. It's a must to have on hand, and will keep for two weeks in the refrigerator.

INGREDIENTS
1 cup heavy cream (not
    ultrapasteurized)
1 cup sour cream

1. Whisk heavy cream and sour cream together and cover loosely with a lid.
2. Let sit in a warm kitchen for 24 hours, and then chill for at least 4 hours before using.

Desserts

Fruit Desserts

★★★★★★★★★★★★★★★ Fruit Crunch ★★★★★★★★★★★★★★★

Submitted by Senator Ernest F. Hollings
From the Kitchen of Mrs. Ernest F. Hollings

★

Ernest F. Hollings

SERVES 6–8

Senator Ernest F. Hollings is a Democrat and represents the state of South Carolina.

INGREDIENTS

6 cups cut-up fresh (pitted and peeled)
   fruit: apples, peaches, cherries
1 cup flour
1½ cups sugar
1 teaspoon baking powder
½ teaspoon salt

1 egg, beaten
½ cup butter, melted
Cinnamon
Nutmeg
Sour cream or ice cream

1. Preheat oven to 350°.
2. Place fruit in a 9-inch square greased baking dish.
3. Combine dry ingredients and stir in egg until thoroughly moistened. Sprinkle this mixture over fruit.
4. Pour melted butter over this.
5. Sprinkle with cinnamon and nutmeg.
6. Bake for 50–60 minutes, or until golden brown.
7. Serve warm or at room temperature, with sour cream or ice cream.

★★★★★★★★★★★★★★ Curried Fruit ★★★★★★★★★★★★★★

Submitted by Representative Ralph M. Hall

SERVES 6–8

Congressman Ralph M. Hall is a Democrat and represents the 4th District of Texas.

INGREDIENTS

1 16-ounce can peach halves

1 16-ounce can pear halves

1 16-ounce can apricots

1 16-ounce can pineapple chunks

1 10-ounce jar red cherries

¾ cup brown sugar

2 teaspoons curry powder

1 tablespoon cinnamon

½ teaspoon nutmeg

½ cup butter or margarine

1. Preheat oven to 350°.
2. Combine fruit in a casserole or baking dish.
3. Bring to boil brown sugar, curry powder, cinnamon, nutmeg, and butter.
4. Pour mixture over fruit.
5. Bake for 20 minutes. Serve warm.

★★★★★★★★★★★ **Apple Crumble** ★★★★★★★★★★★

Submitted by Senator Paul Sarbanes
From the Kitchen of Christine Sarbanes

SERVES 6–8

66 *This is our family's favorite dessert, and comes from England."*
—Senator Paul Sarbanes is a Democrat and represents the state of Maryland.

Preparation Tip: This is also good made with other fruit such as blueberries, peaches, etc. Serve with a small jug of heavy cream (unwhipped).

INGREDIENTS

1½ pounds large cooking apples, peeled
  and cored
3–4 tablespoons sugar
Juice of ½ lemon
¼ teaspoon cinnamon

¼ pound butter
2 cups flour
½ cup sugar
¼ teaspoon ground ginger

1. Preheat oven to 350°.

2. Cut apples into eighths.

3. Mix apples with sugar, lemon juice, and cinnamon in a 1-quart glass baking dish.

4. In a mixing bowl, cream butter into flour until it is the consistency of fine bread crumbs.

5. Add sugar and ground ginger, and mix in well.

6. Sprinkle the crumble over the apples and press down lightly.

7. Bake until golden brown and apples are cooked, 30–40 minutes.

★

Paul Sarbanes

★★★★★★★★★★★★★ **Baked Apples** ★★★★★★★★★★★★★

Submitted by Senator John D. Rockefeller IV

SERVES 4

*S*enator John D. Rockefeller IV is a Democrat and represents the state of West Virginia.

INGREDIENTS

4 Granny Smith apples
2 tablespoons sugar
4 teaspoons butter or margarine
¼ cup raisins

⅓ cup brown sugar, firmly packed
1 tablespoon flour
½ teaspoon cinnamon
1 tablespoon water

1. Preheat oven to 375°.

2. Lightly grease the bottom of a small rectangular glass baking dish with margarine or butter.

3. Core apples to within ½ inch of the bottom, and peel away skin from around top of apple. Slice a small piece from bottom of apple so that it will stand up straight in baking dish. Place apples in baking dish.

4. Mix sugar and butter with raisins and place in cored-out cavity of each apple.

5. Bake for approximately 20 minutes.

6. Meanwhile, in a small bowl, combine brown sugar, flour, cinnamon, and water.

7. Spoon over baked apples and continue baking for 10 more minutes.

8. Serve either warm or cool.

Cakes

✱✱✱✱✱✱✱✱✱ **Banana-Pineapple Cake** ✱✱✱✱✱✱✱✱✱

Submitted by Representative Steven Schiff
From the Kitchen of Marcia Schiff

SERVES 8–10

Congressman Steven Schiff is a Republican and represents the 1st District of New Mexico.

INGREDIENTS

3 cups sifted flour	1½ cups liquid cooking oil
1 teaspoon baking soda	1¼ teaspoons vanilla
1 teaspoon cinnamon	3 eggs, beaten
2 cups sugar	1 8-ounce can crushed pineapple
1 teaspoon salt	1 cup chopped pecans or walnuts
2 cups diced ripe bananas	(optional)

1. Preheat oven to 350°.

2. Sift dry ingredients into a large bowl.

3. Add bananas, oil, vanilla, eggs, and crushed pineapple with juice. Stir to blend (do not beat).

4. Pour into a greased and floured 9-inch tube pan and bake for 1 hour and 20 minutes.

5. Cool and remove from pan.

★★★★★★★★★★★ **Cherry Nut Bread** ★★★★★★★★★★★★

Submitted by Representative Tim Johnson
From the Kitchen of Barbara Johnson

SERVES 6–8

Congressman Tim Johnson is a Democrat and represents, at large, the state of South Dakota.

INGREDIENTS

8 ounces cream cheese
1 cup margarine
1½ cups sugar
1½ teaspoons vanilla
4 eggs

2¼ cups sifted flour
1½ teaspoons baking powder
¾ cup cherries
½ cup chopped pecans

Glaze:
1½ cups powdered sugar
2 tablespoons milk

1. Preheat oven to 325°.
2. Thoroughly blend cream cheese, margarine, sugar, and vanilla.
3. Add eggs one at a time, mixing well after each addition.
4. Sift 2 cups flour with baking powder and mix in gradually.
5. Combine remaining flour and cherries and add nuts. Fold into batter.
6. Grease 10-inch loaf or Bundt pan. Pour batter into pan.
7. Bake for 1 hour and 20 minutes.
8. Cool 5 minutes, then remove from pan.
9. Combine glaze ingredients and drizzle over cake.

★★★★★★★★★★ **Our Family Gingerbread** ★★★★★★★★★★

Submitted by Senator Bob Smith
From the Kitchen of Mary Jo Smith

SERVES 6–8

S enator Bob Smith is a Republican and represents the state of New Hampshire.

INGREDIENTS

1 cup shortening or margarine
1 cup dark molasses
1 cup sugar
1 cup sour milk (milk with 1 tablespoon
   lemon juice or vinegar added)
1 egg, well beaten

1 teaspoon baking soda, dissolved in 2
   teaspoons boiling water
Pinch of salt
2¼ cups flour
2 teaspoons ginger

1. Preheat oven to 300°–325°.
2. Bring shortening, molasses, and sugar to a boil and set aside.
3. Mix sour milk, egg, baking soda dissolved in water, and salt together and add to molasses mixture.
4. Sift flour and ginger together and add to original mixture.
5. Pour into a greased 9 x 9 x 2 baking pan and bake for 45–60 minutes.

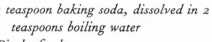

175

★

Bob Smith

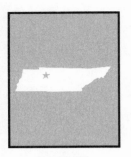

Ruth Thompson's Fresh Coconut Cake
★★★★★★★★ **with Fluffy White Frosting** ★★★★★★★★

Submitted by Senator Fred Thompson
From the Kitchen of Ruth Thompson

SERVES 8–10

*S*enator Fred Thompson is a Republican and represents the state of Tennessee.

INGREDIENTS

½ cup vegetable shortening
1¼ cups granulated sugar
2 cups sifted cake flour
2½ teaspoons baking soda
¼ teaspoon salt
1 cup milk
1 teaspoon vanilla extract
3 egg whites
Meat of 1 fresh coconut, grated, milk
    reserved

Fluffy White Frosting:

1⅔ cups granulated sugar
½ cup water
¼ teaspoon cream of tartar
½ cup egg whites (3)

1. Preheat oven to 350°.
2. Cream shortening and sugar in a large bowl until fluffy.
3. Sift flour, baking powder, and salt together, 3 times. Then, alternating with milk, add dry ingredients to creamed shortening small amounts at a time, beating until smooth after each addition.
4. Add vanilla.
5. Beat egg whites until they peak, then stir into batter.
6. Bake in 2 greased and floured 8- or 9-inch cake pans for 30 minutes, or until done.
7. Let cool. Dribble coconut milk over each layer before frosting.

Frosting:

  1. Combine sugar, water, and cream of tartar in a small saucepan; stir over low heat until sugar is dissolved.

  2. Boil without stirring until syrup threads from spoon.

  3. Beat egg whites until stiff.

  4. Add syrup gradually, beating all the time, until cool enough to spread.

  5. Frost top and sides of cake.

  6. Sprinkle coconut on top and sides of cake.

★

Fred Thompson

✴✴✴✴✴✴✴✴✴✴✴ # Maple Syrup Cake ✴✴✴✴✴✴✴✴✴✴✴

Submitted by Senator Jim Jeffords

SERVES 8–10

❝*A*n old favorite Vermont recipe of mine.*"*
     —*Senator James M. Jeffords is a Republican and represents the state of Vermont.*

INGREDIENTS

½ cup shortening
½ cup white sugar
2 eggs, beaten lightly
1 cup Vermont maple syrup grade A dark
   amber
¼ cup water

2½ cups cake flour
½ teaspoon ginger
¼ teaspoon baking soda
2 teaspoons baking powder
Maple icing (optional)
Walnut halves (optional)

1. Preheat oven to 325°.

2. Cream shortening, adding sugar gradually.

3. Sift flour, measure, then sift again with ginger, baking soda, and baking powder added.

4. Beat eggs, maple syrup, and water into creamed shortening.

5. Add dry ingredients gradually to wet, beating until smooth.

6. Bake in a tube pan about 50 minutes. Let cool 15 minutes in pan, then invert onto a serving plate.

7. If desired, cover with maple icing and decorate with nut halves. You may try your local gourmet bake shop for maple icing, or add a few drops of maple flavoring to vanilla frosting.

✶✶✶✶✶✶✶✶ **Deep Dark Chocolate Cake** ✶✶✶✶✶✶✶✶

Submitted by Representative Sam Brownback

SERVES 8–10

*C*ongressman *Sam Brownback is a Republican and represents the 2nd District of Kansas.*

Sam Brownback

INGREDIENTS

1¾ cups flour	*1 teaspoon salt*
2 cups sugar	*2 eggs*
¾ cup cocoa powder	*2 teaspoons vanilla*
1½ teaspoons baking soda	*½ cup vegetable oil*
1½ teaspoons baking powder	*1 cup boiling water*

1. Preheat oven to 350°.

2. Combine dry ingredients in large bowl.

3. Add eggs, vanilla, and oil.

4. Beat with electric beater on medium speed 2 minutes.

5. Stir in boiling water. Batter will be thin.

6. Pour into greased and floured pans (2 9-inch or 3 8-inch layer pans, or 1 13 x 9 pan).

7. Bake at 350° for 30–35 minutes for layers; 35–40 minutes for 13 x 9 pan. Cake is done when a toothpick inserted in the center comes out dry. Cool. Frost with favorite icing. Can use two 8-inch pans and make some mini-muffins or cupcakes, also.

✭✭✭✭✭ Chocolate Huckleberry Layer Cake ✭✭✭✭✭

Submitted by Senator Conrad Burns

SERVES 8–10

❝*The following recipe has been a favorite of mine for years.*❞
—*Senator Conrad Burns is a Republican and represents the state of Montana.*

Preparation Tip: You may substitute blueberries for the huckleberries. Instead of using chocolate cake mix, you can make your own chocolate cake from scratch, or use a moist pudding-cake mix.

INGREDIENTS
1 package chocolate cake mix

Filling:
2 tablespoons tapioca
½ cup water
1 tablespoon lemon juice
2 cups huckleberries
¼ cup sugar
⅛ teaspoon salt

Fudge Frosting:
½ cup softened margarine or butter
2 cups powdered sugar
½ teaspoon vanilla
¼ cup half-and-half or condensed milk
⅜ cup cocoa powder

1. Make 2 rounds chocolate cake according to package directions.

Filling:

1. Combine tapioca, water, and lemon juice. Let stand 10 minutes.
2. Combine with huckleberries, sugar, and salt in microwave-safe bowl.
3. Microwave on high for 5 minutes, stirring every 1 minute.
4. Spread between cooled layers of chocolate cake.

Frosting:

1. Cream margarine.
2. Blend in 1 cup powdered sugar.
3. Blend in vanilla and half-and-half.
4. Add cocoa and remaining powdered sugar and combine. Stir until smooth, adding additional milk or sugar if necessary to reach desired consistency.
5. Cover cake with frosting.

★

Conrad Burns

★★★★★★★★★★★★ Carrot Cake ★★★★★★★★★★★★

Submitted by Senator Carl Levin

SERVES 8–10

*S*enator Carl Levin is a Democrat and represents the state of Michigan.

Preparation Tip: This recipe is geared for a food processor; however, it can be adapted to an electric mixer.

INGREDIENTS

1 cup flour
¾ cup sugar
1 teaspoon baking powder
½ teaspoon cinnamon
½ teaspoon salt
2 eggs
⅝ cup oil
1 cup grated carrots
1 8-ounce can crushed pineapple
½ cup roughly chopped walnuts

Frosting:

3 ounces butter
3 ounces cream cheese
½ teaspoon vanilla
3 heaping tablespoons confectioner's sugar

1. Preheat oven to 350°.
2. Put all dry ingredients in food processor and process 5–10 seconds.
3. Add eggs and oil and process 30 seconds (will be very thick).
4. Add carrots and pineapple and mix thoroughly.
5. Add nuts and mix only to distribute.
6. Bake in greased 9 x 11 pan about 1 hour. Cool.

Frosting:

1. Put butter, cheese, and vanilla in food processor and process about 20 seconds. Add sugar and continue processing until thoroughly combined and smooth.
2. When cake is cold, pat frosting all over top.

★★★★★ Tom Daschle's Famous Cheesecake ★★★★★

Submitted by Senator Tom Daschle

SERVES 6–8

66 *This recipe is a favorite of the Daschle family because it calls for many of the ingredients found on South Dakota Farms!"*
—Senator Tom Daschle is a Democrat and represents the state of South Dakota.

183

★

Tom Daschle

INGREDIENTS

½ cup sugar
2 8-ounce packages cream cheese
4 eggs, beaten
1½ cups sour cream
Juice of 1 lemon
1 teaspoon vanilla extract
1 teaspoon almond extract

Crust:

⅓ cup crushed graham crackers
1 stick butter, melted
¼ cup sugar

1. Preheat oven to 375°.
2. Combine all crust ingredients in a large bowl, blend thoroughly, and press into a springform pan.
3. Cream together sugar and cream cheese in a large bowl.
4. Fold in eggs.
5. Add remaining ingredients and combine thoroughly.
6. Pour batter into crust and bake for 20 minutes, until cheesecake rises and turns golden brown.
7. Let cool at room temperature and then refrigerate several hours before serving.
8. Delicious served by itself or smothered in berries of your choice.

★★★★★★★★★★★ Italian Cream Cake ★★★★★★★★★★★

Submitted by Representative John T. Myers

SERVES 8–10

Congressman John T. Myers is a Republican and represents the 7th District of Indiana.

INGREDIENTS

1 stick butter
½ cup shortening
2 cups sugar
1 teaspoon vanilla
5 egg yolks
2 cups flour

1 teaspoon baking soda
1 cup buttermilk
3 egg whites
1 7-ounce can shredded coconut; reserve 2
    tablespoons for topping
1 cup chopped pecans

Frosting:

1 8-ounce package cream cheese
½ stick butter
1 teaspoon vanilla
1 16-ounce box powdered sugar

1. Preheat oven to 350°.
2. Cream first 4 ingredients together.
3. Add egg yolks, one at a time, and beat well after each addition.
4. Sift together flour and baking soda. Add to yolk mixture alternately with buttermilk, beating after each addition until smooth.
5. Beat egg whites until very stiff, then fold in.
6. Stir in coconut and ½ cup chopped pecans.
7. Pour into 3 well-greased and floured 8-inch cake pans.
8. Bake for 30 minutes, or until done and brown. Let cool.

Frosting:

1. Beat cream cheese and butter together, add vanilla and powdered sugar, and beat until smooth and creamy.

2. When cake is cool, spread frosting between layers, around sides, and on top.

3. Sprinkle remaining chopped pecans and 2 tablespoons coconut on top.

185

★

John T. Myers

✮✮✮✮✮✮✮✮✮ Light Strawberry Cake ✮✮✮✮✮✮✮✮✮✮

Submitted by Senator Robert F. Bennett

SERVES 12

Senator Robert F. Bennett is a Republican and represents the state of Utah.

Preparation Tip: De-fat your cake mixes by replacing the oil with an equal amount of applesauce. Also, replace each egg with two egg whites. Use nonstick cooking spray to grease pans. The original recipe for this cake was 395 calories per serving, with 21 grams of fat. This revised recipe has 218 calories per serving, with 3 grams of fat.

INGREDIENTS

1 box light white cake mix
16 ounces frozen unsweetened
   strawberries, thawed, mashed, and
   drained; liquid reserved
½ cup water

3 egg whites
1 teaspoon strawberry extract
2 tablespoons reserved strawberry liquid
½ cup powdered sugar

1. Preheat oven to 350°.
2. Spray a 9 x 13 glass baking dish with nonstick cooking spray.
3. Place cake mix in a large mixing bowl and add strawberries, water, egg whites, and extract.
4. Blend with hand electric beater on low speed for 30 seconds.
5. Beat on medium speed for 2 minutes, scraping sides of bowl with rubber spatula. Pour into prepared pan.
6. Bake 30 minutes, until top springs back when touched lightly.
7. Combine reserved strawberry liquid with powdered sugar and pour evenly over warm cake.

★★★★★★★★★★★★ **Fresh Apple Cake** ★★★★★★★★★★★★

Submitted by Representative John Tanner

Serves 10–12

Congressman John Tanner is a Democrat and represents the 8th District of Tennessee.

INGREDIENTS

½ cup canola oil

2 cups sugar

3 eggs, beaten

2½ cups all-purpose flour

½ teaspoon salt

¾ teaspoon baking soda

1 tablespoon baking powder

1 tablespoon cinnamon

1 tablespoon ground cloves

3 cups diced peeled apples (York or
    Granny Smith preferred)

1–2 cups chopped pecans and/or walnuts

1–2 tablespoons vanilla extract

1. Preheat oven to 325°.
2. Blend oil, sugar, and eggs in a large bowl.
3. Combine dry ingredients, add to wet ingredients, and mix well.
4. Add apples, pecans, and vanilla and stir well.
5. Pour into 9-inch tube pan which has been generously buttered and floured.
6. Cook for 1 hour and 15 minutes.
7. Cool cake in pan for 15 minutes, then invert onto a serving plate.

187

★

John Tanner

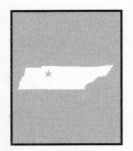

★★★★★★★★ **Cream Cheese Pound Cake** ★★★★★★★★

Submitted by Representative John Tanner

SERVES 10–12

Congressman John Tanner is a Democrat and represents the 8th District of Tennessee.

INGREDIENTS

3 sticks butter, at room temperature

1 8-ounce package cream cheese, at room temperature

3 cups sugar

½ teaspoon salt

1 tablespoon almond flavoring

1 teaspoon vanilla

6 large eggs, at room temperature

3 cups sifted all-purpose flour

1. Preheat oven to 325°.

2. Cream butter, cream cheese, and sugar together until light and fluffy.

3. Add salt, almond flavoring, and vanilla to this mixture.

4. Add eggs, beating well after each addition.

5. Beat in flour.

6. Grease and flour a 9-inch tube pan, or spray with nonstick cooking spray, and pour in batter.

7. Bake for about 1 hour. Watch that it doesn't brown too quickly on top before the inside is done. Cover top with a loose sheet of aluminum foil when desired brownness is reached, then continue baking.

Freezes well.

★★★★★★★★★ **Nannie's Molasses Cake** ★★★★★★★★★

Submitted by Representative Bill Baker
From the Kitchen of Joanne Baker

SERVES 10–12

" *A recipe that has been in my wife, Joanne's, family for a number of generations."*
—*Congressman Bill Baker is a Republican and represents the 10th District of California.*

189
★
Bill Baker

INGREDIENTS

2 teaspoons baking soda
1 cup hot water
1 cup white sugar
½ cup molasses
½ cup shortening

2 cups flour
2 teaspoons cinnamon
1 teaspoon ginger
2 eggs, beaten
1 cup raisins

1. Preheat oven to 325°.
2. Dissolve baking soda in hot water.
3. Beat all remaining ingredients together.
4. Stir in hot water/baking soda mixture.
5. Pour batter into a greased 9 x 11 baking pan.
6. Bake for 25–35 minutes.

★★★★★★★★★★★★★ Lemon Cake ★★★★★★★★★★★★★★★

Submitted by Representative Doug Bereuter

SERVES 6

ongressman Doug Bereuter is a Republican and represents the 1st District of Nebraska.

INGREDIENTS

½ cup flour
¼ teaspoon salt
1¼ cups sugar
3 eggs, separated

Grated peel and juice of 2 large lemons
2 tablespoons butter, melted
1½ cups milk
1 cup heavy cream, whipped

1. Preheat oven to 375°.
2. Sift flour, salt, and 1 cup sugar together into a mixing bowl.
3. Beat egg yolks slightly, and stir into dry ingredients along with lemon peel, lemon juice, and butter.
4. Add milk and mix thoroughly.
5. Beat egg whites until foamy, gradually add remaining ¼ cup sugar, and beat until stiff. Fold into lemon mixture, turn into an ungreased 2-quart baking dish, and set into a pan of hot water (about 1 inch deep).
6. Bake for 30–40 minutes, or until top is browned and knife inserted halfway in center comes out clean.
7. Spoon into serving dishes while warm. Top with whipped cream.

★★★★★★★★★★★ Lemon Jell-O Cake ★★★★★★★★★★★★

Submitted by Senator Russell Feingold
From the Kitchen of Sylvia Feingold

SERVES 8–10

*S*enator Russell Feingold is a Democrat and represents the state of Wisconsin.

INGREDIENTS

1 3-ounce package of lemon Jell-O
1 cup boiling water
¾ cup vegetable oil
1 box of yellow cake mix (8.4 ounces,
   approximately, depending on brand)

4 eggs
1 cup powdered sugar
Juice of one large lemon

1. Preheat oven to 350°.

2. Dissolve Jell-O in 1 cup boiling water. Cool.

3. Add oil to cake mix, beat well. Add eggs, one at a time, beating well after each addition.

4. Add cooled lemon Jell-O. Beat well. Pour into greased 9 x 13 pan and bake for 40 minutes at 350°. Test with toothpick. Cake is done when toothpick comes out clean.

5. When done, remove from oven and prick with fork while still hot. Mix powdered sugar and lemon juice and drizzle over warm cake.

6. Cut into squares and serve.

★

Russell Feingold

✶✶✶✶✶✶ **Muskingum Chocolate Dew Cake** ✶✶✶✶✶✶

Submitted by Senator John Glenn
From the Kitchen of Annie Glenn

SERVES 10–12

❝*John Glenn has always liked a moist cake! This is the one our children requested for special occasions such as birthdays. For one who really enjoys chocolate, a chocolate icing on this cake just can't be beaten. Enjoy!*❞
—Annie Glenn, wife of Senator John Glenn. Senator Glenn is a Democrat and represents the state of Ohio.

INGREDIENTS

2 cups sifted cake flour
1 cup sugar
4 tablespoons cocoa powder
½ teaspoon salt
2 teaspoons baking soda

1 teaspoon vanilla
1 cup cold water
1 cup mayonnaise
Chocolate icing (optional)

1. Preheat oven to 350°.
2. Sift flour, sugar, cocoa, salt, and baking soda together several times.
3. Add vanilla and mix well.
4. Add cold water and mayonnaise and mix together well.
5. Pour into 2 greased 8-inch cake pans.
6. Bake for 30 minutes; test for doneness with toothpick.
7. Serve as is, or spread with your favorite chocolate icing.

★★★★★★★★★★★★ **Lemon Flip Cake** ★★★★★★★★★★★★

Submitted by Senator Richard Lugar

SERVES 6–8

$\mathcal{S}$enator Richard Lugar is a Republican and represents the state of Indiana.

INGREDIENTS

1 tablespoon butter
2 tablespoons flour
¾ cup sugar, scant

2 eggs, separated
¼ cup freshly squeezed lemon juice
1 cup milk

1. Preheat oven to 350°.
2. Cream butter, flour, and sugar.
3. Beat egg yolks and add with lemon juice and milk.
4. Beat egg whites until stiff, then fold in.
5. Bake in ungreased 8-inch baking dish set in a pan of water for 35 minutes.
6. When cool, flip cake over onto a plate.
7. Sauce (custard consistency) is now on the top.

★

Richard Lugar

★★★★★★ Apple Cake with Caramel Icing ★★★★★★

Submitted by Representative Tim Hutchinson

SERVES 8–10

Congressman Tim Hutchinson is a Republican and represents the 3rd District of Arkansas.

INGREDIENTS

2¼ cups sugar
1 cup oil
3 eggs
1 teaspoon vanilla
3 cups flour
1 teaspoon baking soda
1 teaspoon baking powder
1 heaping teaspoon cinnamon
½ teaspoon salt
4 cups finely chopped peeled apples
1 cup chopped pecans

Caramel Icing:

1 cup sugar
½ stick margarine
½ teaspoon baking soda
½ teaspoon vanilla
1 tablespoon white corn syrup
½ cup buttermilk

1. Preheat oven to 350°.
2. Mix sugar and oil.
3. Beat in eggs and vanilla.
4. Sift dry ingredients together.
5. Add to sugar mixture. Dough should be very stiff.
6. Add apples and nuts and mix well.
7. Pour into ungreased 9 x 13 baking pan.
8. Bake for 1 hour.

Icing:

1. Mix ingredients.
2. 15 minutes before cake is done, begin cooking over medium heat until mixture becomes caramelized.
3. Pour icing over cake.

Pies

✶✶✶✶✶✶✶✶✶✶ Key Lime Yogurt Pie ✶✶✶✶✶✶✶✶✶✶

Submitted by Senator Connie Mack

SERVES 6–8

*T*his recipe comes from The Good Book of Nutrition.* *A variation of the Key West speciality, the filling is sweetened with apple juice concentrate and flavored with Key limes.*
—Senator Connie Mack is a Republican and represents the state of Florida.

INGREDIENTS

1¼ cups graham cracker crumbs
2 tablespoons corn oil margarine, melted
½ cup frozen apple juice concentrate, thawed
1¼-ounce envelope unflavored gelatin
⅓ cup granulated sugar

⅓ cup fresh lime juice
2 teaspoons freshly grated lime rind
¼ teaspoon vanilla extract
1½ cups low-fat plain yogurt
Key lime slices

1. In a small bowl, combine crumbs and margarine; mix well.

2. Press crumb mixture over bottom and sides of a 9-inch pie plate. Freeze.

3. Pour apple juice into a saucepan. Sprinkle with gelatin and let stand for several minutes, or until gelatin is softened.

4. Add sugar and cook over low heat until gelatin and sugar dissolve, stirring constantly.

5. Pour gelatin mixture into bowl of electric mixer.

*Nashville, Tenn.: Great American Opportunities, 1987. Recipe contains approximately per serving: 152 calories; 4.6 grams of fat; 27.23 percent calories from fat. Used with the permission of the American Cancer Society.

6. Add lime juice, rind, and vanilla.
7. Chill until mixture resembles raw egg whites. Beat until fluffy.
8. Add yogurt; beat until fluffy.
9. Pour yogurt mixture into prepared crust. Chill until firm, about 2 hours.
10. Garnish with lime slices.

✶✶✶✶✶✶✶✶✶✶ New Mexico Apple Pie ✶✶✶✶✶✶✶✶✶✶

Submitted by Representative Joe Skeen

SERVES 6–8

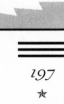

*C*ongressman Joe Skeen is a Republican and represents the 2nd District of New Mexico.

Preparation Tip: If you are not fortunate enough to live in New Mexico, you may make substitutions for the apples and pistachios. Select apples that are locally grown, as we did.

197

✶

Joe Skeen

INGREDIENTS

2 cups cooked sliced Hondo Valley (New Mexico) apples
2 tablespoons flour
¾ cup sugar
Pinch of salt
1 egg
1 teaspoon vanilla
1 cup sour cream
1 9-inch pie shell, unbaked

Topping:

⅓ cup sugar
⅓ cup flour
1 teaspoon cinnamon
4 teaspoons soft butter
Finely chopped Alamogordo (New Mexico) pistachio nuts

1. Preheat oven to 350°.
2. Mash apples slightly; add flour, sugar, and salt.
3. Beat egg and vanilla together and add to apple mixture.
4. Beat sour cream until stiff and fold into apple mixture.
5. Pour into pie shell and bake for 40 minutes.
6. Remove pie. Mix topping ingredients and sprinkle onto pie top. Return to oven for 15 minutes.

★★★★★★★★★★★★★★ Parfait Pie ★★★★★★★★★★★★★★

Submitted by Representative James B. Longley, Jr.
From the Kitchen of Mrs. James B. Longley

SERVES 6–8

66 *A quick and easy dessert."*
—*Senator James B. Longley, Jr., is a Republican and represents the 1st District of Maine.*

Preparation Tip: This recipe can also be done with strawberry Jell-O and strawberries.

INGREDIENTS

1 package lime Jell-O
1 8-ounce can crushed pineapple
Hot water
1 pint vanilla ice cream

1 9-inch graham cracker pie shell, or
   baked pastry shell
1 cup heavy cream, whipped (or Cool
   Whip works well)

1. Dissolve Jell-O in juice from pineapple plus enough hot water to make 1 ¼ cups liquid. Stir well.

2. While still hot, add ice cream and stir until ice cream melts.

3. Let stand until shaky, then fold in well-drained pineapple and pour into pie shell.

4. Keep in refrigerator until serving time, then frost with whipped cream.

✶✶✶✶✶✶✶✶✶ **Melba Glock's Peach Pie** ✶✶✶✶✶✶✶✶✶

Submitted by Senator J. Robert Kerrey
From the Kitchen of Melba Glock

SERVES 6–8

" *A Nebraska farm wife, Melba Glock is a dear friend of Senator Kerrey's; he's always happy to enjoy her legendary peach pie.* "
—*Senator J. Robert Kerrey is a Democrat and represents the state of Nebraska.*

199

✶

J. Robert Kerrey

INGREDIENTS

4 cups sliced peaches
¾ cup sugar
4 tablespoons flour, or 2 tablespoons
   cornstarch
¼ teaspoon almond extract
1 tablespoon margarine

Pastry:

2 cups flour
1 teaspoon salt
¼ cup cold water
¾ cup vegetable shortening

Prepare Pastry:

1. Sift and measure flour. Sift again with salt.
2. Take out ⅓ cup flour and mix to a paste with cold water.
3. Cut shortening into remaining flour until mixture is crumbly.
4. Stir in paste and mix with a fork until dough follows fork in one piece.
5. Knead slightly, cover with damp towel, and place in refrigerator until cool.

Assemble Pie:

1. Preheat oven to 375°.
2. Place sliced peaches in mixing bowl, mix together sugar and flour and blend with peaches.
3. Roll out pastry for bottom and top pie crusts.

4. Line a 9-inch pie plate with pastry. Add almond flavoring to peach mixture and pour into pie pan. Dot with margarine.

5. Moisten edge of pastry with water and cover with top crust. Seal and make openings in crust to allow steam to escape.

6. Bake for 40–50 minutes.

★★★★★★★★★★★★★★★ **Chess Pie** ★★★★★★★★★★★★★★★

Submitted by Representative John Tanner

SERVES 6–8

*C*ongressman John Tanner is a Democrat and represents the 8th District of Tennessee.

INGREDIENTS

3 eggs, beaten
1½ cups sugar
¼–½ cup milk
1 stick butter, melted
2 teaspoons flour

1 tablespoon cornmeal
1½ teaspoons vanilla
Dash of salt
1 9-inch pie crust, unbaked

1. Preheat oven to 350°.
2. Combine first 8 ingredients.
3. Pour into pie shell and bake for 35–45 minutes.
4. Because butter browns quickly, you may want to cover pie loosely with aluminum foil when filling reaches desired brownness while rest of pie finishes baking.

201

★

John Tanner

✭✭✭✭✭✭✭✭✭✭✭✭✭✭ **Ice Box Pie** ✭✭✭✭✭✭✭✭✭✭✭✭✭✭

Submitted by Senator Nancy Landon Kassebaum

SERVES 6–8

"*This easy dessert has long been a family favorite, and I hope it will be a hit at your home, too!*"
—*Senator Nancy Landon Kassebaum is a Republican and represents the state of Kansas.*

INGREDIENTS

3 squares semisweet chocolate, grated
⅓ stick butter
2 cups Rice Krispies

1 pint ice cream (such as Toffee Crunch), (softened)
Grated semisweet chocolate for topping

1. Melt chocolate with butter.
2. Stir in Rice Krispies.
3. Press mixed ingredients into a buttered 10-inch pie plate.
4. Fill with ice cream, and top with additional grated chocolate.
5. Freeze.
6. For easier cutting, take out of freezer 15–30 minutes before serving.

★★★★★★★★★★★★ **Key Lime Pie** ★★★★★★★★★★★★

Submitted by Representative Porter Goss

SERVES 6–8

66 *Florida is famous for its Key limes, and they make one of the best pies. The recipe I'm sharing with you is one of my favorites."*
—Congressman Porter Goss is a Republican and represents the 14th District of Florida.

203
★

Porter Goss

INGREDIENTS

2½ cups condensed milk
¼ cup plus ½ tablespoon freshly squeezed
    Key lime juice
¼ cup plus ½ tablespoon freshly squeezed
    lime juice

3 egg yolks
1 8-inch graham cracker pie crust

1. Preheat oven to 350°.
2. Blend milk and lime juices. Mix very well.
3. Add egg yolks. Mix well.
4. Pour into prepared crust and bake for 12–15 minutes.
5. Pie is done when small dimples appear around edge. Do not overbake.

✶✶✶✶✶✶✶✶ **Lemon Blossom Chiffon Pie** ✶✶✶✶✶✶✶✶

Submitted by Representative Nancy L. Johnson

SERVES 6–8

*C*ongresswoman Nancy L. Johnson is a Republican and represents the 6th District of Connecticut.

INGREDIENTS

½ cup sugar

1¼-ounce envelope unflavored gelatin

⅔ cup water

⅓ cup freshly squeezed lemon juice

4 egg yolks, slightly beaten

1 tablespoon grated lemon rind

1 9-inch pie shell, baked

Whipped cream

Meringue:

4 egg whites

½ teaspoon cream of tartar

½ cup sugar

1. Blend sugar, gelatin, water, lemon juice, and egg yolks thoroughly in saucepan. Cook over medium heat, stirring constantly, until mix just comes to a boil.

2. Stir in grated lemon rind.

3. Place pan in cold water; cool until mixture mounds slightly when dropped from a spoon.

4. For meringue, whip egg whites until stiff. Whip in cream of tartar and sugar gradually until mixture is very stiff.

5. Fold meringue into lemon mixture.

6. Pile into cool baked shell. Chill several hours or overnight.

7. Serve with whipped cream.

✮✮✮✮✮✮✮✮ **South Carolina Pecan Pie** ✮✮✮✮✮✮✮✮✮✮

Submitted by Senator Strom Thurmond

SERVES 6–8

*S*enator Strom Thurmond is a Republican and represents the state of South Carolina.

INGREDIENTS

3 eggs
1 cup dark brown sugar
1 cup light corn syrup
1 tablespoon margarine, melted

⅛ teaspoon salt
1 teaspoon vanilla extract
1 cup chopped pecans
1 9-inch pastry shell, unbaked

1. Preheat oven to 350°.
2. Beat eggs, adding sugar gradually.
3. Add syrup, margarine, salt, vanilla, and pecans and combine.
4. Pour into pastry shell.
5. Bake for 1 hour.

205

✮

Strom Thurmond

********** **Chocolate Chess Pie** **********

Submitted by Senator Jesse Helms
From the Kitchen of Dorothy Helms

SERVES 5–6

Senator Jesse Helms is a Republican and represents the state of North Carolina.

INGREDIENTS

2 eggs, beaten
1 teaspoon vanilla
Dash of salt
1 cup sugar

1 stick butter or margarine
1 square unsweetened chocolate
1 9-inch pie crust, unbaked
Whipped cream

1. Preheat oven to 350°.
2. Blend together eggs, vanilla, salt, and sugar.
3. Melt butter and chocolate together and combine with egg mixture.
4. Pour into crust and bake for 25–30 minutes.
5. Top with whipped cream and serve.

★★★★★★★★★★ **Georgia Pecan Pie** ★★★★★★★★★★

Submitted by Senator Sam Nunn
From the Kitchen of Colleen Nunn

Sam Nunn

SERVES 6–8

"*My own favorite. . . .*"
—*Senator Sam Nunn is a Democrat and represents the state of Georgia.*

INGREDIENTS

1¼ cups sugar
½ cup light corn syrup
¼ cup butter or margarine
3 eggs, slightly beaten

1 cup coarsely chopped pecans
1 teaspoon vanilla
1 9-inch pastry shell, unbaked

1. Preheat oven to 350°.
2. Combine sugar, syrup, and butter in a 2-quart saucepan. Bring to a boil on high, stirring constantly until butter is melted.
3. Remove from stove and gradually add hot syrup to eggs; stir all the while.
4. Add pecans to mixture and cool to lukewarm.
5. Add vanilla.
6. Pour into pie shell and bake for 40–45 minutes.

208

★

Desserts

★★★★★★★★★★★ **Chocolate Chip Pie** ★★★★★★★★★★★★

Submitted by Senator Byron Dorgan

SERVES 6–8

❝*I hope those who receive this recipe enjoy it as much as my family and I do.*❞

—*Senator Byron Dorgan is a Democrat and represents the state of North Dakota.*

INGREDIENTS

30 marshmallows
½–¾ cup milk
2 squares bitter chocolate, grated fine
1 cup whipping cream, whipped
Grated bitter chocolate for topping
   (optional)
Maraschino cherries (optional)

Crust:

10 graham crackers, rolled fine
1 tablespoon butter, softened

1. To prepare crust, mix graham crackers with butter and press into a 9-inch pie pan very firmly, covering both sides and bottom.

2. Melt marshmallows with milk (use double boiler to prevent scorching), and cool.

3. Fold grated chocolate into whipped cream; fold mixture into marshmallow mixture.

4. Pour filling into crust.

5. Decorate with additional grated chocolate and maraschino cherries if you like.

6. Refrigerate overnight or for at least 3–4 hours before serving.

★★★★★★ **My Favorite Black Raspberry Pie** ★★★★★★

Submitted by Senator Mike DeWine

SERVES 6–8

Senator Mike DeWine is a Republican and represents the state of Ohio.

INGREDIENTS

Pastry for 2-crust 9-inch pie

4 cups black raspberries

⅔ cup sugar

¼ cup flour

2 tablespoons butter

1. Preheat oven to 375°.
2. Line 9-inch pie plate with pastry.
3. Fill with raspberries.
4. Mix sugar and flour and sprinkle over berries. Dot with butter.
5. Add top crust. Make slit in top.
6. Bake for 40–45 minutes.

209

★

Mike DeWine

The Maple-Vail Book *Composition Services*

Date: 08-20-96 07:49:04   Job ID: G49233$$34

Connecticut Yankee
★★★★★★★★ **Strawberry-Rhubarb Pie** ★★★★★★★★★

Submitted by Senator Christopher J. Dodd

SERVES 6–8

❝❝ *One of the great joys of Connecticut living is anticipating the bounty of our delicious locally grown food. The enclosed recipe, one of my favorites, combines two of Connecticut's favorite crops in one dish. I'm sure others will enjoy it as much as I do!"*
—*Senator Christopher J. Dodd is a Democrat and represents the state of Connecticut.*

INGREDIENTS
1½ cups sugar
¼ cup all-purpose flour
¼ teaspoon salt
¼ teaspoon freshly grated Connecticut
    nutmeg
3 cups rhubarb, cut into ½-inch pieces
1 cup sliced fresh strawberries
1 tablespoon butter

Crust:
2 cups all-purpose flour
1 teaspoon salt
⅔ cup plus 2 tablespoons butter
6–7 tablespoons very cold water

Prepare Pie Crust:

1. Preheat oven to 350°.
2. Combine butter, flour, and salt. Mix well with a fork.
3. Slowly add 4 tablespoons very cold water as mixing. Add rest of water if necessary until dough is manageable and can be molded into a ball. When this is possible, set aside half the dough for upper crust or lattice top. Wrap in a damp dish towel to keep moist. (Preparation of top should be last step before baking.)
4. With other half of dough, roll out a piece large enough to line a 9-inch pie plate.
5. Prick it with tines of a fork several times. Bake for 7–10 minutes.

Prepare Filling:

1. Mix first 4 ingredients.
2. Combine strawberries and rhubarb with flour mixture, being certain they mix well.
3. Let stand for about 20 minutes.

Assemble Pie:

1. Turn oven up to 400°.
2. When ready, pour filling into prepared shell. Dot with butter.
3. Roll out top crust or lattice strips.
4. Cover pie with top crust or lattice. Moisten edges and seal. If using top crust, prick it with tines of a fork several times. Bake for 40–50 minutes. Serve and enjoy!

211

★

Christopher J. Dodd

Cookies

********* **Snicker Doodle Cookies** **********

Submitted by Senator Dale Bumpers

MAKES ABOUT 3 DOZEN COOKIES

Senator Dale Bumpers is a Democrat and represents the state of Arkansas.

INGREDIENTS

2-¾ cups flour

2 teaspoons cream of tartar

1 teaspoon baking soda

½ teaspoon salt

1 cup (2 sticks) margarine

1½ cups sugar

2 eggs, beaten until creamy

2 tablespoons sugar

1 teaspoon cinnamon

1. Preheat oven to 400°.
2. Sift together flour, cream of tartar, baking soda, and salt.
3. Combine margarine, sugar, and eggs.
4. Add dry ingredients to moist ingredients and mix thoroughly. Chill 2 hours.
5. Combine sugar and cinnamon, and roll teaspoonfuls of dough in mixture.
6. Place 2 inches apart on ungreased cookie sheet. Bake 8–10 minutes.

★★★★★★ **John Warner's Favorite Cookies** ★★★★★★

Submitted by Senator John Warner

MAKES 2–3 DOZEN COOKIES

S enator *John Warner is a Republican and represents the state of Virginia.*

INGREDIENTS

½ pound butter

1 cup brown sugar

¾ cup granulated sugar

2 eggs, beaten

1 teaspoon vanilla

1½ cups flour

1 teaspoon baking soda

1 cup flaked coconut

1½ cups semisweet chocolate chips

¼ cup chopped dates

½ cup sunflower seeds

¼ cup chopped almonds

1. Preheat oven to 325°.

2. Cream butter and add sugar, eggs, and vanilla.

3. Stir in flour and baking soda until thoroughly moistened; add remaining ingredients and combine.

4. Drop spoonfuls of dough onto ungreased baking sheets.

5. Bake for 12 minutes.

213

★

John Warner

214
★

Desserts

★★★★★★★★★★ **Maple-Oatmeal Cookies** ★★★★★★★★★★

Submitted by Senator Judd Gregg
From the Kitchen of Kathy Gregg

MAKES ABOUT 2 DOZEN COOKIES

*S*enator Judd Gregg is a Republican and represents the state of New Hampshire.

Preparation Tip: Grade A dark amber maple syrup is more desirable in cooking than the lighter Fancy grade, as it has a more robust flavor.

INGREDIENTS

1 cup flour
¼ teaspoon salt
1 teaspoon baking powder
1 cup quick-cooking oats
½ cup chopped walnuts

½ cup shortening
1 egg
¾ cup maple syrup (Grade A dark
  amber)
½ teaspoon vanilla

1. Preheat oven to 400°.
2. Mix flour, salt, baking powder, oats, and nuts together.
3. Cream shortening, add egg, and beat until light and fluffy.
4. Add syrup and vanilla, and mix well.
5. Add dry ingredients to wet and mix well.
6. Drop by teaspoonful onto greased cookie sheet.
7. Bake 8–12 minutes.

★★★★ **Grandmother Robb's Oatmeal Cookies** ★★★★

Submitted by Senator Charles S. Robb

MAKES 20 DOZEN COOKIES

66*A favorite Robb family recipe which comes from his mother."
—Senator Charles S. Robb is a Democrat and represents the state of Virginia.*

Preparation Tip: This recipe makes *lots* of cookies. You may cut the recipe in half if you like.

INGREDIENTS

1 pound brown sugar
1 cup white sugar
1½ cups shortening
2 cups flour
2 eggs
1 teaspoon salt (rounded)
6 teaspoons cinnamon (level)

1 teaspoon nutmeg (level)
1 teaspoon baking soda (level)
2 teaspoons baking powder (level)
1 pound raisins
6 cups oatmeal/rolled oats (not instant)
1 cup milk
1 teaspoon vanilla

1. Preheat oven to 350–375°.

2. Mix all ingredients except oatmeal, milk, and vanilla first, being sure they are well blended, using an electric mixer. (Hand mixing is fine too, but an electric mixer is a little easier.)

3. Add rolled oats to batter and when they are blended in, add milk and vanilla.

4. Drop by teaspoonful (or use a cookie press) onto a lightly greased (or sprayed with nonstick cooking spray) cookie sheet.

5. Bake for 15–20 minutes; much depends on the individual oven. Remove when they begin to lightly brown, otherwise they'll become too hard.

215
★

Charles S. Robb

Grandmother Merrick's
★★★★★★★★★★ Soft Molasses Cookies ★★★★★★★★★★★

Submitted by Senator William Cohen

MAKES 2–3 DOZEN COOKIES

66 *O ne of my family's favorite recipes."*
—*Senator William Cohen is a Republican and represents the state of Maine.*

INGREDIENTS

⅓ cup shortening
½ cup boiling water
1 teaspoon salt
¾ cup molasses
½ cup granulated sugar
1 egg

2½ cups sifted all-purpose flour
2 teaspoons baking powder
½ teaspoon baking soda
1 teaspoon ginger
1 teaspoon cinnamon

1. Preheat oven to 375°.

2. Place shortening in a bowl. Pour in boiling water and add salt.

3. Stir in molasses, sugar, and unbeaten egg, and beat well.

4. Sift flour together with baking powder, baking soda, ginger, and cinnamon. Stir into molasses mixture.

5. Drop by spoonfuls onto greased cookie sheet.

6. Bake for 12–15 minutes.

⊛ther Sweets

Submitted by Representative Barbara Cubin

MAKES 48 BARS

Congresswoman Barbara Cubin is a Republican and represents, at large, the state of Wyoming.

Preparation Tip: If you don't have fresh buttermilk on hand, substitute 2 teaspoons vinegar or lemon juice mixed into ½ cup milk. Or you may use powdered buttermilk mixed according to package directions. The coffee can be replaced with 1 cup of water if desired.

217
★

Barbara Cubin

INGREDIENTS

2 cups all-purpose flour
2 cups granulated sugar
½ cup butter
½ cup shortening
1 cup strong brewed coffee
¼ cup dark, unsweetened cocoa powder
½ cup buttermilk
2 eggs, beaten
1 teaspoon baking soda
1 teaspoon vanilla

Frosting:

½ cup butter (1 stick)
2 tablespoons dark cocoa powder
¼ cup milk
3½ cups powdered sugar
1 teaspoon vanilla

1. Preheat oven to 400°.

2. In a large mixing bowl, combine flour and sugar.

3. In a heavy saucepan, combine butter, shortening, coffee, and cocoa. Stir and heat to boiling. Pour boiling mixture over the flour and sugar in bowl.

4. Add buttermilk, eggs, baking soda, and vanilla. Mix well, using a wooden spoon or a high speed electric mixer.

5. Pour into a well-buttered 17½ x 11 jelly roll pan. Bake for 20 minutes, or until brownies test done in the center. While brownies bake, prepare frosting.

Frosting:

1. In a saucepan, combine butter, cocoa, and milk. Heat to boiling, stirring constantly.
2. Mix in powdered sugar and vanilla until frosting is smooth.

Finishing:

1. Pour warm frosting over brownies as soon as you take them out of oven.
2. Cool and then cut up into 48 bars.

✭✭✭✭✭✭✭✭ **Double Chocolate Brownies** ✭✭✭✭✭✭✭✭

Submitted by Senator Sam Nunn

SERVES 8–10

$\mathcal{S}$enator Sam Nunn is a Democrat and represents the state of Georgia.

INGREDIENTS

¾ cup all-purpose flour
¼ teaspoon baking soda
¼ teaspoon salt
⅓ cup butter
¾ cup sugar
2 tablespoons water

1 teaspoon vanilla
1 12-ounce package semisweet chocolate
 chips
2 eggs
½ cup chopped pecans

1. Preheat oven to 325°.
2. In a small bowl, combine flour, baking soda, and salt. Set aside.
3. In a small saucepan, combine butter, sugar, and water; bring just to a boil. Remove from heat. Add vanilla and half the chocolate chips. Stir until melted and mixture is smooth. Transfer to a large bowl.
4. Add eggs, one at a time, beating after each addition. Gradually blend in flour mixture.
5. Stir in nuts and remaining chocolate chips.
6. Pour into a greased 9-inch square baking pan. Bake for 40–45 minutes.

Sam Nunn

✱✱✱✱✱✱✱✱✱ Light Brownie Pudding ✱✱✱✱✱✱✱✱✱

Submitted by Senator Robert F. Bennett

SERVES 6–8

*S*enator Robert F. Bennett is a Republican and represents the state of Utah.

INGREDIENTS

1 cup flour
½ teaspoon salt
2 tablespoons cocoa powder
2 teaspoons baking powder
¾ cup sugar
½ cup milk
1 teaspoon vanilla
2 tablespoons margarine, melted
½–1 cup chopped nuts

Sauce:

¾ cup brown sugar
¼ cup cocoa powder
1¾ cups hot water

1. Preheat oven to 350°.

2. Sift together flour, salt, cocoa, baking powder, and sugar.

3. To this mixture add milk, vanilla, margarine, and nuts. Mix thoroughly.

4. Pour into 8-inch square pan.

5. To prepare sauce, in a separate bowl, mix sauce ingredients until melted. Pour over batter. Sauce will seep to bottom of brownies during cooking.

6. Bake for 40–50 minutes.

7. Cut into squares and invert onto serving dishes, so sauce is on top.

★★★★★★★★★★★★★★★ **French Mint** ★★★★★★★★★★★★★★★

Submitted by Senator Orrin Hatch

SERVES 24

66 *This is a delicately mint-flavored frozen dessert, and is my favorite dessert recipe.*"

—*Senator Orrin Hatch is a Republican and represents the state of Utah.*

INGREDIENTS

4 1-ounce squares unsweetened chocolate,
    or 1 6-ounce package chocolate chips
1 cup soft butter
2 cups powdered sugar

4 eggs
1 teaspoon vanilla
1 teaspoon peppermint extract
Chopped nuts

1. Melt chocolate. Cool and set aside.

2. Using an electric beater, beat butter while gradually adding sugar (about 15 minutes).

3. Add cooled melted chocolate. Beat 5 minutes more.

4. Beat in eggs, one at a time. Mix in vanilla and peppermint extract.

5. Sprinkle chopped nuts on bottom of 24 cupcake holders in cupcake pan. Fill each cupcake holder half full with batter. Sprinkle more nuts on top.

6. Freeze for at least 3 hours.

★★★★★★★ **Hungarian Rhapsody Dessert** ★★★★★★★

Submitted by Representative Tom Lantos
From the Kitchen of Annette Lantos

SERVES 18–22

Congressman Tom Lantos is a Democrat and represents the 12th District of California.

INGREDIENTS

1½ cups butter or margarine
1⅓ cups sugar
8 eggs, separated
3 teaspoons freshly squeezed lemon juice,
   or vanilla
⅓ cup flour
2 8-ounce packages cream cheese

Crust:

1 cup melted butter
½ cup powdered sugar
2 cups flour

1. Preheat oven to 350°.

2. To prepare crust, mix melted butter, powdered sugar, and flour, pat into 9 x 13 Pyrex dish, and bake 20 minutes. Leave oven on for final baking.

3. While crust is baking, prepare filling. Cream together butter with 1 cup sugar. Add egg yolks, one at a time, beating well after each addition. Add lemon juice or vanilla, flour, and cream cheese. Cream until smooth.

4. Whip egg whites, gradually adding remaining ⅓ cup sugar. Fold into egg yolk mixture.

5. Pour into "half-baked" crust. Bake 35–45 minutes. Test with knife to see if it comes out clean.

6. Dust with powdered sugar. Cut into small squares.

May be frozen.

★★★★★★★ Cousin Susie's Perfect Fudge ★★★★★★★

Submitted by Senator Kay Bailey Hutchison

SERVES 10—12

66 *These are some of my favorite recipes.* They keep me from being homesick for Texas while I am in Washington.*"

—*Senator Kay Bailey Hutchison is a Republican and represents the state of Texas.*

INGREDIENTS

1 6-ounce package semisweet chocolate chips, and *6-ounce package butterscotch chips* or *1 12-ounce package milk chocolate chips*

1 14-ounce can condensed milk
½ teaspoon vanilla
1 cup chopped pecans (optional)

1. Combine chips and milk and microwave on high for 2½ minutes.

2. Stir and microwave for 2½ minutes more.

3. Add vanilla and pecans.

4. Pour into a greased 9 x 11 glass baking pan and refrigerate for at least one hour before serving.

223
★

Kay Bailey Hutchison

*Other recipes from Senator Hutchison appear on pages 140 and 224.

Ray Hutchison's Homemade
★★★★★★★★★★★★ Vanilla Ice Cream ★★★★★★★★★★★★

Submitted by Senator Kay Bailey Hutchison

MAKES 1 GALLON ICE CREAM

$\mathcal{S}$enator Kay Bailey Hutchison is a Republican and represents the state of Texas.

Preparation Tip: These ingredients are for a 1-gallon freezer; increase or reduce proportionately for ½- or 1½-gallon freezers.

INGREDIENTS

4 eggs
4 cups sugar
1 pint half-and-half
1 pint whipping cream

1 .35-ounce box vanilla Junket
1 14-ounce can condensed milk
2 teaspoons vanilla
Whole milk to fill freezer

1. Blend eggs, sugar, half-and-half, and whipping cream in an electric mixer until sugar dissolves.

2. Dissolve Junket in a small amount of whole milk and add to mixture.

3. Add condensed milk and vanilla and blend until mixture is smooth.

4. Pour into freezer can. Fill to capacity with whole milk and freeze according to freezer directions.

Index

Agnew, Judy, 16, 17
Agnew, Spiro T., 16, 17
Akaka, Daniel K., 50, 58
Alabama, 39, 53, 155
Alaska, 76
Amy Adam's lemon chicken, 49
appetizers:
    cheese straws, 155
    garbanzo dip, 159
    hot chicken wings à la Thomas, 156
    hot crab-artichoke dip, 158
    hot crab dip, 160
    Josefinas, 154
    keftedes (Greek meatballs), 25
    miniature ham rolls, 153
    tostada grande, 157
apple:
    baked, 172
    cake, fresh, 187
    cake with caramel icing, 194
    crumble, 171
    fruit crunch, 169
    pie, New Mexico, 197
    popovers, giant, 149
    soup, Missouri, 132
Archer, Bill, 41
Arizona, 94

Arizona baked beans, 94
Arkansas, 33, 135, 194, 212
artichoke-crab dip, hot, 158
Aunt Evelyn's johnnycake or muffins, 145
award-winning chili, Senator Gramm's, 95

baked:
    apples, 172
    lima beans, 97
    rice, 102
    shad and roe, 78
Baker, Bill, 189
Baker, Joanne, 189
banana:
    blu'bana bread, 12
    bread, quick and easy, 114
    -pineapple cake, 173
barbecue(d):
    chicken, 5
    sauce, 5
bars, salted nut, 15
bean(s):
    Arizona baked, 94
    Cincinnati chili, 96
    garbanzo dip, 159
    hoppin' John, 93
    lentil soup, 128

bean(s): *(continued)*
    lima, baked, 97
    and rice, searchlight, 98
    salad, Dakota, 23
    soup, the famous Senate Restaurant, 130
    stew, Dakota, 23
beef:
    "bohemian" teriyaki, 29
    broil, lite and lean, 21
    Cincinnati chili, 96
    Dakota bean salad, 23
    Dakota bean stew, 24
    Exon family favorite casserole, 30
    extra-meaty lasagna, 121
    Grandma Daigle's rice dressing, 100
    keftedes (Greek meatballs), 25
    marinated eye of the round, 26
    Senator Gramm's award-winning chili, 95
    Sherry's spaghetti sauce and meatballs, 122
    South Dakota taco salad, 27
    Swedish meatballs, 28
    wild rice stew, 21
beets in sour cream sauce, 90
Bennett, Robert F., 43, 186, 220
Bereuter, Doug, 62, 190
Bernice, potato à la, 85
berries:
    blu'bana bread, 12
    chocolate huckleberry layer cake, 180
    Connecticut Yankee strawberry-rhubarb pie, 210–11
    light strawberry cake, 186
    my favorite black raspberry pie, 209
    red, white, and blue cobbler, 7
    strawberry-spinach salad, 105
Bilirakis, Michael, 25, 75, 87
black raspberry pie, my favorite, 209
blu'bana bread, 12
blueberry:
    blu'bana bread, 12
    red, white, and blue cobbler, 7
Boehlert, Sherwood, 122
Boehner, John A., 105
"bohemian" teriyaki beef, 29
Bond, Caroline, 132
Bond, Christopher, 132
braised pork chops, 64
bread:
    Aunt Evelyn's johnnycake or muffins, 145
    corn, easy, 112
    corn, the Grassley family's favorite, 111

    monkey, 10
    Swedish rye, 115
bread, sweet:
    blu'bana, 12
    cherry-nut, 174
    Georgia peach, 113
    quick and easy banana, 114
    zucchini nut, 116
Breaux, John, 100
broccoli:
    salad, 107
    soup, cream of, with no cream, 11
broil(ed):
    lite and lean beef, 21
    pork chops, 64
Brownback, Mary, 116
Brownback, Sam, 116, 179
brownies:
    double chocolate, 219
    pudding, light, 220
    Texas, 217
Bumpers, Dale, 135, 212
Burns, Conrad, 180
Bush, Barbara, 5, 7, 9
Bush, George, 5, 7, 9, 14

cabbage, stuffed, 88
cake:
    apple, with caramel icing, 194
    banana-pineapple, 173
    carrot, 182
    chocolate huckleberry layer, 180
    cream cheese pound, 188
    deep dark chocolate, 179
    fresh apple, 187
    Italian cream, 184
    lemon, 190
    lemon flip, 193
    lemon Jello, 191
    light strawberry, 186
    maple syrup, 178
    Muskingum chocolate dew, 192
    Nannie's molasses, 189
    our family gingerbread, 175
    Ruth Thompson's fresh coconut, with fluffy white frosting, 176
    Tom Daschle's famous cheesecake, 183
Calautti, Lucy, 123
California, 37, 73

Camire, Jeannette, 57
Cape Cod fish chowder, Senator Ted Kennedy's, 141
carrot cake, 182
Carter, Jimmy, 11, 15
Carter, Rosalynn, 11
Caruso chicken and rice, 36
casserole:
    catfish, 71
    Exon family favorite, 30
    hash brown, 84
    pizza, 119
    shrimp-squash, 13
catfish casserole, 71
Chafee, John H., 114, 138, 145
Charleston she-crab soup, 129
cheese:
    Josefinas, 154
    straws, 155
cheesecake, Tom Daschle's famous, 183
cherry:
    fruit crunch, 169
    -nut bread, 174
    red, white, and blue cobbler, 7
chess pie, 201
    chocolate, 206
chicken:
    barbecued, 5
    breast dinner, 42
    Caruso and rice, 36
    curried, Mrs. Sheila Wellstone's, 40
    Dottie Miller's Oriental, 48
    -garlic phyllo rolls, 37
    grilled pesto-stuffed, with lemon butter, 41
    honey-mustard, 47
    Korean, 50
    lemon, Amy Adam's, 49
    peachy, 34
    picatta, Marty Meehan's, 46
    salad, fruited, 45
    salad, Oriental, 33
    salad, Senator J. Bennett Johnston's favorite, 35
    scallopini, 44
    sweet and sour (low-fat), 43
    Tetrazzini, 39
    velvet soup, 134
    wings à la Thomas, hot, 156
chiffon pie, lemon blossom, 204
chili:
    Cincinnati, 96

Senator Gramm's award-winning, 95
chocolate:
    brownies, double, 219
    cake, deep dark, 179
    chess pie, 206
    chip pie, 208
    chips, Hillary Clinton's, 3
    cousin Susie's perfect fudge, 223
    dew cake, Muskingum, 192
    French mint, 221
    huckleberry layer cake, 180
    Texas brownie, 217
chops, pork:
    braised or broiled, 64
    pepper, 61
    and Spanish rice, 59
    stuffed Iowa, 63
chowder:
    clam, 138
    easy hearty corn, 140
    Rhode Island clam, 139
    Senator Ted Kennedy's Cape Cod fish, 141
Christmas Tortière (pork pie), 57
chutney, Indian green, 164
cilantro and lime grilled turkey breast in pita pockets, 51
clam chowder, 138
    Rhode Island, 139
Clinton, Bill, 3, 4
Clinton, Hillary, 3
cobbler:
    peach, 14
    red, white, and blue, 7
coconut cake with fluffy white frosting, Ruth Thompson's fresh, 176
coffee punch, Liz Bryant's, 163
Cohen, William, 216
cole slaw, 9
Colorado, 120
Connecticut, 101, 204, 210–11
Connecticut Yankee strawberry-rhubarb pie, 210–11
Conrad, Kent, 123
cookies:
    Grandmother Merrick's soft molasses, 216
    Grandmother Robb's oatmeal, 215
    Hillary Clinton's chocolate chips, 3
    maple-oatmeal, 214
    Senator John Warner's favorite, 213
    snicker doodle, 212
    see also brownies

corn, tamale, 86
corn bread:
  Aunt Evelyn's johnnycake or muffins, 145
  easy, 112
  the Grassley family's favorite, 111
corn chowder, easy hearty, 140
Cortner, Bettye, 64
cousin Susie's perfect fudge, 223
Coverdell, Paul D., 42
crab cakes, Senator John Warner's Norfolk, 77
crab dip, hot, 160
  artichoke-, 158
crab soup:
  Charleston she-, 129
  Dale's, 135
Craig, Larry E., 21
Craig, Suzanne, 21
Crane, Philip M., 90
cream cake, Italian, 184
cream cheese pound cake, 188
cream of broccoli soup with no cream, 11
crème fraîche, 16
crumble, apple, 171
crunch, fruit, 169
Cubin, Barbara, 83, 86, 217
curried:
  chicken, Mrs. Sheila Wellstone's, 40
  fruit, 170

Dakota bean salad, 23
Dakota bean stew, 24
Dale's crab soup, 135
D'Amato, Alfonse, 44, 61, 89, 102, 121, 127, 128
D'Amato, Antoinette, 44, 61, 89, 121, 127, 128
Daschle, Tom, 27, 183
Davis, Sallie, 158, 160
deep dark chocolate cake, 179
Delaware, 78
dentist's dream French toast, 147
dessert:
  apple cake with caramel icing, 194
  apple crumble, 171
  baked apples, 172
  banana-pineapple cake, 173
  carrot cake, 182
  cherry-nut bread, 174
  chess pie, 201
  chocolate chess pie, 206
  chocolate chip pie, 208

chocolate huckleberry layer cake, 180
Connecticut Yankee strawberry-rhubarb pie, 210–11
cousin Susie's perfect fudge, 223
cream cheese pound cake, 188
curried fruit, 170
deep dark chocolate cake, 179
French mint, 221
fresh apple cake, 187
fruit crunch, 169
Georgia pecan pie, 207
grape juice fruit ice, 17
Hungarian rhapsody, 222
ice box pie, 202
Italian cream cake, 184
Key lime pie, 203
Key lime yogurt pie, 195
lemon blossom chiffon pie, 204
lemon cake, 190
lemon flip cake, 193
lemon Jello cake, 191
light strawberry cake, 186
maple syrup cake, 178
Melba Glock's peach pie, 199
Muskingum chocolate dew cake, 192
my favorite black raspberry pie, 209
Nannie's molasses cake, 189
New Mexico apple pie, 197
our family gingerbread, 175
parfait pie, 198
peach cobbler, 14
Ray Hutchinson's homemade vanilla ice cream, 224
red, white, and blue cobbler, 7
Ruth Thompson's fresh coconut cake, with fluffy white frosting, 176
salted nut bars, 15
South Carolina pecan pie, 205
Tennessee treats, 4
Tom Daschle's famous cheesecake, 183
see also brownies; cookies
DeWine, Mike, 209
Dijon, fish, 69
dill-potato soup, 133
dip:
  garbanzo, 159
  hot crab, 160
  hot crab-artichoke, 158
Dodd, Christopher, 210–11
Dole, Bob, 74
Dooley, Calvin, 37

Dorgan, Byron, 208
Dottie Miller's Oriental chicken, 48
double chocolate brownies, 219
dove on the grill, 53
dressing:
    Grandma Daigle's rice, 100
    sesame, 165

easy hearty corn chowder, 140
English scones, Mom's, 148
Exon, J. James, 29, 30
Exon, Patricia, 29, 30
Exon family favorite casserole, 30
extra-meaty lasagna, 123

Faircloth, Lauch, 64
famous Senate Restaurant bean soup, the, 130
Feingold, Russell, 191
Feingold, Sylvia, 191
Feinstein, Dianne, 73
fish:
    baked shad and roe, 78
    catfish casserole, 71
    chowder, Senator Ted Kennedy's Cape Cod fish, 141
    Dijon, 69
    red snapper, 72
    sautéed trout with fresh tarragon, 70
    see also seafood
Florida, 25, 34, 48, 49, 69, 75, 87, 163, 195, 203
Ford, Betty, 12
Ford, Gerald, 12
Frank's favorite scallops, 76
French-cut string beans, 89
French mint, 221
French toast, dentist's dream, 147
fresh apple cake, 187
frittata, pasta, 120
fruit:
    crunch, 169
    curried, 170
    fruited chicken salad, 45
    see also specific fruits
fudge, cousin Suzie's perfect, 223

garbanzo dip, 159
garithes me lemoni ke lathee (shrimp with lemon and olive oil),
    75
garlic-chicken phyllo rolls, 37
Georgia, 42, 72, 107, 113, 159, 207, 219

Georgia peach bread recipe, 113
Georgia pecan pie, 207
giant apple popovers, 149
gingerbread, our family, 175
Glenn, Annie, 192
Glenn, John, 192
Glock, Melba, 199
Gonzalez, Henry B., 59
Good Book of Nutrition, The, 34, 69, 195
Gore, Al, 4
Gore, Tipper, 4
Goss, Porter, 203
Gramm, Phil, 95
Grandma Daigle's rice dressing, 100
Grandmother Merrick's soft molasses cookies, 216
Grandmother Robb's oatmeal cookies, 215
grape:
    juice fruit ice, 17
    soup, 136
Grassley, Charles E., 111
Grassley family's favorite corn bread, 111
Greek meatballs (keftedes), 25
green chutney, Indian, 164
Gregg, Judd, 214
Gregg, Kathy, 214
grilled:
    pesto-stuffed chicken with lemon butter, 41
    turkey breast in pita pockets, lime and cilantro, 51

Hall, Ralph, 170
ham rolls, miniature, 154
Harkin, Tom, 63
hash brown casserole, 84
Hatch, Orrin, 221
Hawaii, 50, 58
Heflin, Elizabeth, 39, 155
Heflin, Howell, 39, 155
Helms, Dorothy, 206
Helms, Jesse, 97, 206
Hillary Clinton's chocolate chips, 3
Hollings, Ernest F., 129, 169
Hollings, Rita, 169
honey-mustard chicken, 47
hoppin' John, 93
hot chicken wings à la Thomas, 156
hot crab dip, 160
    artichoke-, 158
huckleberry chocolate layer cake, 180
Hungarian rhapsody dessert, 222

Hutchison, Kay Bailey, 140, 223
Hutchison, Tim, 194

ice, grape juice fruit, 17
ice box pie, 202
ice cream, Ray Hutchison's homemade vanilla, 224
Idaho, 21, 85, 130
Illinois, 90
Indiana, 51, 154, 158, 160, 165, 184, 193
Indian green chutney, 164
Inhofe, James, 148, 166
Inhofe, Kay, 166
instant meatball soup, 127
Iowa, 63, 84, 111
Iowa pork chops, stuffed, 63
Italian cream cake, 184

Jeffords, James M., 178
Jello cake, lemon, 191
johnnycake, Aunt Evelyn's, 145
Johnson, Barbara, 174
Johnson, Lady Bird, 13
Johnson, Lyndon, 13
Johnson, Nancy L., 204
Johnson, Tim, 174
Johnston, J. Bennett, 35
Josefinas, 154

Kansas, 74, 116, 179, 202
Kassebaum, Nancy Landon, 202
keftedes (Greek meatballs), 25
Kempthorne, Dirk, 85
Kennedy, John F., 13
Kennedy, Joseph P., II, 147
Kennedy, Ted, 141
Kentucky, 93
Kerrey, J. Robert, 199
Kerry, John, 36
Key lime pie, 203
    yogurt, 195
Korean chicken, 50

lamb, roast leg of spring, 65
Lantos, Annette, 222
Lantos, Tom, 222
Largent, Steve, 45
lasagna, 121
    extra-meaty, 123
Latham, Kathy, 84

Latham, Tom, 84
Lautenberg, Frank, 47
leg of spring lamb, roast, 65
lemon:
    blossom chiffon pie, 204
    cake, 190
    chicken, Amy Adam's, 49
    flip cake, 193
    Jello cake, 191
    shrimp with olive oil and (garithes me lemoni ke lathee), 75
lentil soup, 128
Levin, Carl, 88, 130, 182
Lieberman, Joseph, 101
light:
    brownie pudding, 220
    lima beans, baked, 97
    strawberry cake, 186
lime:
    and cilantro grilled turkey breast in pita pockets, 51
    Key, pie, 203
    Key, yogurt pie, 195
lite and lean beef broil, 21
Liz Bryant's coffee punch, 163
Longley, James B., Jr., 119, 198
Longley, Mrs., 119, 198
Lott, Trent, 71
Louisiana, 35, 100
low-fat sweet and sour chicken, 43
Lugar, Richard, 51, 193

McCain, John, 94
McConnell, Mitch, 93
Mack, Connie, 34, 69, 195
Maine, 119, 198, 216
maple:
    -oatmeal cookies, 214
    syrup cake, 178
marinated eye of the round, 26
Marty Meehan's chicken picatta, 46
Maryland, 171
Massachusetts, 36, 46, 136, 141, 147
meatballs:
    Greek (keftedes), 25
    Sherry's spaghetti sauce and, 122
    soup, instant, 127
    Swedish, 28
Meehan, Marty, 46
Melba Glock's peach pie, 199

Michigan, 88, 130, 182
Milliken, Diane, 57
miniature ham rolls, 153
Minnesota, 40, 130
Mississippi, 71
Missouri, 132
Missouri apple soup, 132
molasses:
    cake, Nannie's, 189
    cookies, Grandmother Merrick's soft, 216
Mom's English scones, 148
Mondale, Joan, 15
Mondale, Walter, 15
monkey bread, 10
Montana, 180
Moynihan, Daniel Patrick, 70, 133
Mrs. Sheila Wellstone's curried chicken, 40
muffins, Aunt Evelyn's, 145
Murkowski, Frank H., 76
Murray, Patty, 146
mushrooms and wild rice, 99
Muskingum chocolate dew cake, 192
Myers, John T., 154, 157, 158, 160, 165
my favorite black raspberry pie, 209

Nannie's molasses cake, 189
Nebraska, 29, 30, 62, 190, 199
Nethercutt, George R., Jr., 99, 134
Nevada, 98
New Hampshire, 107, 175, 214
New Jersey, 47
New Mexico, 173, 197
New Mexico apple pie, 197
New York, 44, 61, 70, 89, 102, 121, 122, 127, 128, 133
Nixon, Richard M., 16, 17
Norfolk crab cakes, Senator John Warner's, 77
North Carolina, 26, 64, 97, 206
North Dakota, 123, 208
Nunn, Colleen, 113, 159, 207
Nunn, Sam, 72, 106, 107, 113, 159, 207, 219
nut:
    bars, salted, 15
    bread, zucchini, 116
    -cherry bread, 174

oatmeal:
    cookies, Grandmother Robb's, 215
    -maple cookies, 214
Ohio, 96, 105, 112, 192, 209

Oklahoma, 45, 148, 166
Olver, Helen Fulleborn, 136
Olver, John W., 136
Oregon, 21
Oriental chicken:
    Dottie Miller's, 48
    salad, 33
our family gingerbread, 175
Oxley, Michael G., 96, 112

Packwood, Bob, 22
pancakes, Swedish, 146
parfait pie, 198
pasta:
    frittata, 120
    lasagna, 121
    pizza casserole, 119
    Sherry's spaghetti sauce and meatballs, 122
peach:
    bread recipe, Georgia, 113
    cobbler, 14
    fruit crunch, 169
    pie, Melba Glock's, 199
peachy chicken, 34
pecan pie:
    Georgia, 207
    South Carolina, 205
Pedersen, Lynda, 15
Pell, Claiborne, 139
Pennsylvania, 65, 79, 149, 164
pepper pork chops, 61
pesto-stuffed chicken with lemon butter, grilled, 41
phyllo rolls, chicken-garlic, 37
pie:
    chess, 201
    chocolate chess, 206
    chocolate chip, 208
    Connecticut Yankee strawberry-rhubarb pie, 210–11
    Georgia pecan, 207
    ice box, 202
    Key lime, 203
    Key lime yogurt, 195
    lemon blossom chiffon, 204
    Melba Glock's peach, 199
    my favorite black raspberry, 209
    New Mexico apple, 197
    parfait, 198
pie, savory:
    pork (Christmas Tortière), 57

pie, savory: *(continued)*
    spinach (spanakopita), 87
pie, South Carolina pecan, 205
pilaf, pistachio rice, 101
pineapple:
    -banana cake, 173
    parfait pie, 198
pistachio rice pilaf, 101
pizza casserole, 119
popovers, giant apple, 149
pork:
    pie (Christmas Tortière), 57
    roast, 62
    Swedish meatballs, 28
    sweet-sour spareribs, 58
pork chops:
    braised or broiled, 64
    pepper, 61
    and Spanish rice, 59
    stuffed Iowa, 63
potato:
    à la Bernice, 85
    -dill soup, 133
    hash brown casserole, 84
    Texas, 83
pound cake, cream cheese, 188
Pressler, Harriet, 23
Pressler, Larry, 23
Pryor, David, 33
pudding, light brownie, 220
punch, Liz Bryant's coffee, 163

Quayle, J. Danforth, 14
Quayle, Marilyn, 14
quick and easy banana bread, 114

raspberry pie, black, my favorite, 209
Ray Hutchison's homemade vanilla ice cream, 224
Reagan, Nancy, 10
Reagan, Ronald, 5, 7, 9
red, white, and blue cobbler, 7
red snapper, 72
Reid, Harry, 98
Rhode Island, 114, 138, 145
Rhode Island clam chowder, 139
rice:
    baked, 102
    and beans, searchlight, 98
    chicken Caruso and, 36
    dressing, Grandma Daigle's, 100

hoppin' John, 93
pilaf, pistachio, 101
Spanish, pork chops and, 59
wild, and mushrooms, 99
wild, stew, 22
Richard, Shelley, 57
roast:
    leg of spring lamb, 65
    pork, 63
Robb, Charles S., 215
Rockefeller, John D., IV, 172
Rose, Charlie, 26
Roth, William V., Jr., 78
Ruth Thompson's fresh coconut cake, with fluffy white frosting, 176
rye bread, Swedish, 115

salad:
    broccoli, 107
    chicken, Senator J. Bennett Johnston's favorite, 35
    cole slaw, 9
    Dakota bean, 23
    dressing, sesame, 165
    fruited chicken, 45
    Oriental chicken, 33
    South Dakota taco, 27
    strawberry-spinach, 105
    vegetable, 106
salted nut bars, 15
San Francisco seasoned shrimp, 73
Santorum, Rick, 65, 79
Sarbanes, Christine, 171
Sarbanes, Paul, 171
sauce:
    barbecue, 5
    crème fraîche, 166
    Indian green chutney, 164
    Sherry's spaghetti, and meatballs, 122
    spaghetti, 16
sautéed:
    shrimp and scallops, 79
    trout with fresh tarragon, 70
scallopini, chicken, 44
scallops:
    Frank's favorite, 76
    and shrimp, sautéed, 79
Schiff, Marcia, 173
Schiff, Steve, 173
Schroeder, Pat, 120
scones, Mom's English, 148

seafood:
    Charleston she-crab soup, 129
    clam chowder, 138
    Dale's crab soup, 135
    easy hearty corn chowder, 140
    Frank's favorite scallops, 76
    garithes me lemoni ke lathee (shrimp with lemon and olive oil), 75
    hot crab-artichoke dip, 158
    hot crab dip, 160
    Rhode Island clam chowder, 139
    San Francisco seasoned shrimp, 73
    sautéed shrimp and scallops, 79
    Senator John Warner's Norfolk crab cakes, 77
    Seville shrimp, 74
    see also fish
searchlight beans and rice, 98
Senate Restaurant bean soup, the famous, 130
Senator Gramm's award-winning chili, 95
Senator J. Bennett Johnston's favorite chicken salad, 35
Senator John Warner's favorite cookies, 213
Senator John Warner's Norfolk crab cakes, 77
Senator Ted Kennedy's Cape Cod fish chowder, 141
sesame dressing, 165
Seville shrimp, 74
shad and roe, baked, 78
Shelby, Richard, 53
Sherry's spaghetti sauce and meatballs, 122
shrimp:
    with lemon and olive oil *(garithes me lemoni ke lathee)*, 75
    San Francisco seasoned, 73
    and scallops, sautéed, 79
    Seville, 74
    -squash casserole, 13
Skeen, Joe, 197
Smith, Bob, 107, 175
Smith, Mary Jo, 107, 175
snapper, red, 72
snicker doodle cookies, 212
soup:
    Charleston, she-crab, 129
    chicken velvet, 134
    clam chowder, 138
    cream of broccoli with no cream, 11
    Dale's crab, 135
    easy hearty corn chowder, 140
    the famous Senate Restaurant bean, 130
    grape, 136
    instant meatball, 127
    lentil, 128

    Missouri apple, 132
    potato-dill, 133
    Rhode Island clam chowder, 139
    Senator Ted Kennedy's Cape Cod fish chowder, 141
    squash, 131
sour cream sauce, beets in, 90
South Carolina, 129, 153, 169, 205
South Carolina pecan pie, 205
South Dakota, 23, 27, 174
South Dakota taco salad, 27
spaghetti sauce, 16
    and meatballs, Sherry's, 122
    see also pasta
spanakopita (spinach pie), 87
Spanish rice, pork chops and, 59
spareribs, sweet-sour, 58
Specter, Arlen, 149, 164
spinach:
    pie (spanakopita), 87
    -strawberry salad, 105
squash:
    -shrimp casserole, 13
    soup, 131
Stenholm, Charles W., 28, 115
Stenholm, Cindy, 28, 115
stew:
    Dakota bean, 24
    wild rice, 22
Stockman, Steve, 131
strawberry:
    cake, light, 186
    -rhubarb pie, Connecticut Yankee, 210–11
    spinach salad, 105
straws, cheese, 155
string beans, French cut, 89
stuffed:
    cabbage, 88
    Iowa pork chops, 63
Swedish:
    meatballs, 28
    pancakes, 146
    rye bread, 115
sweet and sour:
    chicken (low-fat), 43
    spareribs, 58

taco salad, South Dakota, 27
tamale corn, 86
Tanner, John, 187, 188
Tennessee, 187, 188

Tennessee treats, 4
teriyaki beef, "bohemian," 29
Tetrazzini, chicken, 39
Texas, 28, 41, 59, 95, 115, 131, 140, 170, 224
Texas brownies, 217
Texas potatoes, 83
Thomas, Craig, 156
Thomas, Susan, 156
Thompson, Fred, 176
Thompson, Ruth, 176
Thurmond, Strom, 153, 205
Tom Daschle's famous cheesecake, 183
Tortière, Christmas (pork pie), 57
tostada grande, 157
trout with fresh tarragon, sautéed, 70
turkey breast, grilled lime and cilantro, in pita pockets, 51

Utah, 43, 186, 220, 221

vanilla ice cream, Ray Hutchinson's homemade, 224
vegetable salad, 106

velvet chicken soup, 134
Vermont, 178
Virginia, 77, 213
Vordenbaum, Dee, 131

Warner, John, 77, 213
Washington, 99, 134, 146
Weldon, Dave, 48, 49, 163
Weldon, Nancy, 48, 163
Wellstone, Paul David, 40
Wellstone, Sheila, 40
West Virginia, 172
wild rice:
    and mushrooms, 99
    stew, 22
wings, hot chicken, à la Thomas, 156
Wisconsin, 191
Wyoming, 83, 86, 156, 217

zucchini nut bread, 116